Hacking & Tor

The Complete Beginners

Guide To Hacking, Tor, &

Accessing The Deep Web &

Dark Web

Jack Jones

Table Of Contents

Book 3

Tor: Accessing The Deep Web & Dark Web With Tor:

How To Set Up Tor, Stay Anonymous Online, Avoid

NSA Spying & Access The Deep Web & Dark Web

Book One Starts Here

THE COMPLETE BEGINNER'S GUIDE TO COMPUTER

HACKING

HOW TO HACK NETWORKS & COMPUTER SYSTEMS, INFORMATION GATHERING, PASSWORD CRACKING, SYSTEM ENTRY & WIRELESS HACKING

Jack Jones

Hacking

The Complete Beginner's Guide To Computer Hacking: How To Hack Networks & Computer Systems, Information Gathering, Password Cracking, System Entry & Wireless Hacking

Jack Jones

Table of Contents

Introduction

Chapter 1: How Hacking Works

Chapter 2: Hacking Networks and Computer Systems

Chapter 3: Information Gathering

Chapter 4: Using the Data You Gathered

Chapter 5: Password Cracking for Beginners

Chapter 6: Applications to Gain Entry to Systems

Chapter 7: Wireless Hacking

Conclusion

Introduction

Have you always wondered about how hacking works? In the movies, it seems so simple. All you need is some basic information and some kickass software and you can hack any network you like.

In reality, it's not quite as simple as that. Successful hacking is a combination of using the right tools, a well-planned strategy and applying some basic common sense.

In this book, we will go step by step through strategies that work and over the tools you will need to become a successful hacker.

We'll wade through the lingo used by hackers and teach you how you can get your hands on the information that you need to hack different systems.

We go through applications and software that make the task a lot easier for you and how you can determine what passwords are being used.

We end off with a short lesson on wireless hacking.

By the time we are done, you will have the skills you need to hack the networks that you want to.

And, what if you don't want to use these newly acquired skills to acquire information illegally?

Ethical hackers are a subset of hackers that utilize their skills to pinpoint weaknesses in security systems. They can show companies whether or not their systems are vulnerable.

Perhaps this is something that you can start to do – for yourself or your own company. Learning to think like a hacker does will help you to ensure that your own computer network is as secure as possible.

Chapter 1

How Hacking Works

There is something of a mystique about hackers that the world finds interesting. Hackers are portrayed by Hollywood as the cool kid version of geeks. They are portrayed as rebels who break into systems just to prove that they can. As non-conformists.

No information is safe from this Hollywood portrayal of cool kids. All they have to do is to run a piece of software or to punch out some commands on the keyboard to gain access to even the most secure information.

The truth is that it is not quite that simple. Hackers in the real world have to find ways to exploit weaknesses in the security systems of the networks that they are trying to hack.

They have to be able think both laterally and logically to get around top-flight security systems.

The good news is that it is not that hard to learn to become a hacker. You don't have to be the Hollywood rebel or the geeky teenage genius to be able to do so.

You can learn to think like a hacker and learn what tools they use. You can use this information to either get up to mischief on your own or to help secure your own private network. The choice is yours.

Understanding Hackers

The first step is to start understanding what kinds of hackers there are. People get into hacking for a range of different reasons. The first step towards understanding hackers is to understand what kind of hacker they are.

Hackers – A Basic Classification

- **White Hat Hackers**: People who have no intention of actually causing harm or stealing information fall under this category. For the most part, hackers that fall under this category will work in the security industry, testing systems for vulnerability. They look at how easy a system is to hack and work out ways to increase the protection for the system. They will usually ask for permission from the owner of the systems that they plan to hack before they start to attack it. If you have good intentions when it comes to hacking, it is important that you get permission from the system owners before going ahead. Not doing so can land you in hot water.

- **Black Hat Hackers**: Hackers that fall into this category are generally out to cause harm or steal information. They may aim to cause damage to the system by deleting important information as a purely malicious act. They might also look to steal information that they can profit from – such as credit card numbers. One particularly nasty black hat trick is to take over control of a system and prevent the rightful users from accessing it. They then make the system owners pay them to restore control. When people say that you need to protect yourself against hackers, these are the hackers that they are referring to.

- **Gray Hat Hackers**: Like everything else in life, there are various shades between black and white. This kind of hacker usually gets into it out of curiosity or just to prove that they can. They hack without malicious intent and without any desire to act in any manner that is illegal. (Apart from the hack itself, of course.) These hackers often also turn their skills towards helping system owners protect themselves against black hat hackers. The lines fudge a little because they might hack systems without anyone's express consent for reasons of their own.

What Skills You Need as a Hacker

Skilling yourself as a hacker means that you need to understand how computer systems operate. This means an extensive knowledge of programming, operating systems and networking. It means getting to grips with the major operating systems in use, such as Windows and Linux.

Hackers need to have an above-average grasp of these topics because hacking will often mean finding workarounds in different types of systems.

And you will need to keep up with the latest developments in the field as well. Whenever new software comes out, you will need to understand how it works so that you can pinpoint a weakness in it and fully understand how it operates.

Ideally speaking, you need to have a mind that loves problem-solving and you also need staying power, curiosity and perseverance.

Hacking into systems means having to find loopholes in coding and this can be a painstaking and incredibly boring process at times. It could mean poring over pages of code to find a small weakness that can be exploited.

Hacking Jargon

Hackers have their own lingo and you need to learn some of it if you intend to successfully fit into this world.

Here are some common terms that you will need to know:

- **Exploit:** Refers to a technology or tool that helps you to take advantage of system glitches, bugs and other vulnerabilities. Essentially an exploit is an abbreviated code string that lays the weaknesses in the system bare. They can be used to give you admin privileges, access you are not allowed to have, or to cut off access to authorized users. They are usually the first step that black hat hackers will try. Hackers will usually be able to write their own code in this regard but don't worry too much if you cannot do the same. There are a lot of programs out there that offer generic exploits that you can use instead.

- **Threat**: A threat is something that may be used by a hacker to violate the security of a digital system. Hackers who are involved in shoring up security systems will make a point of looking out for these. These again can be highly personalized by the hacker and are fundamentally intended to breach a system.

- **Vulnerability**: This is what a hacker dreams of. A gap in the code, or glitch in the design that makes it possible for them to get in. This could be in the coded software, in the base design or in the implementation of the program itself. These vulnerabilities allow hackers to access the system as and when they please.

- **Target of Evaluation**: When you hear this term, it is referring to the system that is going to be under attack or that needs to be analyzed. Hackers evaluate the T.O.E. in order to see if there are any weaknesses that may be exploited. They also look for data that makes it easier to break into the system or to crack passwords. Depending on what type of hacker you are, this could be to obtain confidential data such as account numbers, etc. or it could be used to find ways to repair the system and make it less vulnerable to attack. White hat hackers will look for ways to prevent black hat hackers from accessing the system.

- **Attack**: If the system is under attack, it means that it has been compromised as a result of the vulnerabilities within it. The hacker has studied the T.O.E. and found a vulnerability. They may then have written and exploit to take advantage of this error. This is why research is so important. The research phase is where the hacker is going to spend most of their time – they need to identify vulnerabilities that they can take advantage of and this can take a while.

How Do I Get an Exploit to the Targeted System?

There are basically two different approaches when it comes to delivering exploits. These include:

Via Remote Access: In this instance, it is not even necessary to be in direct contact with the targeted system. You can send the exploit to any member within the network and gain access that way. This is a remote hack and the type of hack that we expect most hackers would use.

Via Local Access: This is a little more difficult because it means that you need to have had access to the targeted system at some stage in time. It is, however, the method that most seasoned hackers will employ – it is easier to move around in a system that you already have had access to. This is also why people working at companies have only enough access to the systems to allow them to do their job properly. Should they try to change or delete data that falls outside of their ambit, they would be unable to do so.

This system can be effective at reducing the chances of a local exploit. It should also be stated here that the majority of hacks end up being traced to individuals working within the targeted company. This kind of internal hack means getting as much access to the systems as possible, and even building your privilege level so that you have more access.

Chapter 2

Hacking Networks and Computer Systems

If you ask the professionals, there are five different steps that all hacks go through. If you are aiming to be a successful hacker yourself, you need to know each of these steps backwards.

Information Gathering

Researching the target thoroughly is something that expert hackers believe to be extremely important.

Passive Information Gathering

For passive information gathering to be successful, you need to stay under the radar. Your target is not going to know that you are gathering information about them. This could be physical reconnaissance, such as watching when your target leaves for work every day or a form of cyber-stalking.

For a hacker, most passive information gathering will be done online. Start out with a simple search engine search on the name of your target and see what comes up. Pay attention to personal life details – birthdays, pet's names, children's names, etc.

This information can come in useful when it comes to figuring out passwords and usernames or answers to security questions.

If you need information of a more technical nature, you can sniff the network – that is, gather information that is being transmitted over the network. This enables you to find private servers or networks, IP addresses, and other unencrypted data and is usually done with the help of monitoring software.

It's basically the same as watching your target when they go to work or come home. Except that, in this case, you are monitoring the transactions within the system. This allows you to find out when transactions are occurring and what happens to the data that is sent out.

The draw for this type of surveillance is that it is hard to pick up on. There is little chance that your target will realize that this is what is happening.

Active Information Gathering

This involves actually probing the target network to enable you to find the data that you are looking for and to determine what computers are part of the network.

This is very different to passive information gathering and may involve the use of aggressive methods. If the network you are attacking is being properly monitored, these attacks will be picked up. This method thus comes with a much higher chance of getting caught.

Having said that, there is only a certain amount of information that you will be able to gather passively. If you cannot get what you need passively, you are going to need to move into a more active way of gathering information.

This first step is essential if you want to be a truly successful hacker. Without enough information on the system and how it works, you are not going to be able to devise a working strategy to find vulnerabilities in the system.

Scanning

The second step is to make use of the information that you gathered before to make a thorough analysis of the targeted system. Most hackers use the following tools to help with this:

- Dialer

- Ping sweep

- A Port Scanner

- Network mapper

- ICMP Scanner

- SNMP Sweeper

- Vulnerability scanner

A hacker will look for information regarding the software that has been installed, the names and IP addresses of the different computers within the network, information about user accounts and what operating systems are in use.

This information makes it possible for the hacker to establish how best to hack the system, how to avoid being detected, and how to cover their tracks after the fact.

Gaining Access

It is during this stage that the attack actually begins. Weaknesses are exploited during this stage, allowing the hacker to gain access.

The hacker will try to gain entry through physical access to a computer within the system, by gaining access through a computer on the same local area network, or by gaining access via the internet.

There are a number of ways to do this but the primary goal is to gain control of the system. This allows the hacker to access whatever data they want and to control the system. They will usually attempt to block authorized access to the system so that they can maintain control of it.

Keeping Access Open

Once the hack has been successful, the hacker will usually want to leave a doorway open so that they can access the system at will.

Hackers will usually do this by installing software or coding that allows them entry again later. This can be in the form of Trojans, backdoors and rootkits.

The goal this is not only to allow the hacker access to the system again but also to cover up the vulnerabilities that led to them being able to hack the system in the first place. They do not want the system owners to fix these errors and they do not want other hackers to be able to exploit them either.

Maintaining your access to a system can be useful, even if you have taken all the data you want because you can use the hacked system to launch attacks on other systems. The system then becomes known as a zombie system.

Covering Your Tracks

If you are doing something illegal, it makes sense that you want to cover your tracks so that you can avoid prosecution. Depending on the reason for the hack, you may not want anyone to know that the system was hacked. (Hackers that act to cause mayhem or to destroy a system generally want people to know it was hacked, though.)

If, for example, your goal was simply to access confidential information, or you plan to be able to access the system again, you are going to want to cover your tracks.

This may include modifying the log files of the system, and removing or changing all traces of access. It could mean employing steganography, where files are concealed within other files. It could mean using a tunneling protocol, where you are able to add in a protocol that is not necessarily supported by the system.

Technology that You Need to Know About

You are bound to find it surprisingly easy to find tools to help you with hacking online. Installing malware is only one way to gain access to a system. There are a number of different approaches that you can try.

The tools that you might want to look into include:

Applications: Applications are often not checked for vulnerabilities, especially when they are being written. Often an application will be field-tested for bugs and glitches. When the bugs and glitches are detected, patches will be made to fix these. The main drive behind applications is getting the best features in the least amount of time.

This makes things a lot easier for hackers. It means that applications are more likely to have errors that make them more vulnerable to attack.

Misconfigurations: Errors in setups can also be exploited and disguised by hackers to allow them constant access to a particular system.

Shrink-Wrap Code: There are many generic programs out there that have far more features than the average user will ever use. These can be used to gain access to a system. One example is the "Macros" feature in Microsoft Word.

Such features allow hackers to trigger programs from within the application itself.

Operating Systems: Your average user will use the default settings when they install an operating system for the first time. This can give hackers easier access because these settings are not usually designed to protect against network hacks.

Attacks that Hackers May Use

To write a comprehensive list of what techniques hackers may use is beyond the scope of this book. What we will do, however, is to list the most popular techniques. Most hackers will learn a limited number of techniques really well. This expertise helps to make them more efficient at hacking.

It's kind of like a college specialization – you can study medicine and become a GP, for example. But if you want to become an expert in Virology, for example, you will need to specialize and study all you can about that field.

Specialization in a few different techniques assists hackers in becoming experts in those techniques and it is far easier to keep up in advances in one or two techniques than it would be for six or seven techniques.

In addition, it is not very practical to want to master all hacking techniques. They are all complex and take a good deal of practice to perfect.

If you are working with a client to identify potential vulnerabilities, you can ask them what problems they have been having with hackers. This can help narrow down the approach that you use.

Here are some of the most popular points of entry for a hacker:

Through a LAN: In this instance, the hacker needs to get access to the physical network before they are able to start the attack. Wireless networks have made this a little easier as you don't need to physically be on a computer within the network – you can hack the signal. Wireless networks are a hacker's dream as you just need to be within range of the network to hack it and normally do not have to be in the building itself.

Remote Network: These are where you try to gain access to a system through the internet. This is a method that is also popular with hackers as, again, it does not require you to actually have physical access to a computer within the system.

Most companies spend a lot of time and effort to shore up their systems to prevent this kind of attack so you might need to get really creative or be willing to persevere.

Stolen Equipment: This is where a resource such as a laptop or mobile phone that has access to the targeted system is stolen. This is often one of the easiest ways of hacking the system as companies will often go to great lengths to defend their systems against online hacks and not as much against devices used within the organization.

Hackers can get a lot of useful information in this way – passwords, information about the systems, security protocols, etc.

The longer the device is missing without he authorized owner knowing about it, the better for the hacker. Should an employee's personal device be stolen, it must be reported and removed from the network immediately to prevent unauthorized access.

If it is found later, it can always be added back on – in the meantime, however, you just cannot tell who is accessing it.

Remote Dial-Up Network: This technique makes use of the modem pools within the targeted system.

War dialing is a popular line of attack here. War dialing consists of dialing a system over and over again to discover vulnerabilities within that system and is often used to great effect when it comes to hacking a dial-up network.

In order to reduce the risk of this happening, companies who want their data to remain secure have tended to replace their dial-up systems with more secure, internet-based ones.

Social Engineering: When it comes to this method, the hacker looks at trying to find a way to access the system through one of the authorized users on that system. This is slightly riskier as it entails you either meeting someone or calling in so that you can get the information required. It can be useful when you are finding it difficult to crack passwords, are looking for the usernames of targets, and want to learn more regarding the security that the system has in place. This could mean phoning in to check a detail such as an email address. It could also mean befriending someone or finding someone that can be paid to get the information that you want.

Physical Entry: To get this right, you need to physically access the target system. This can be risky as it increases the chances of being caught but it can potentially make the hack much easier. In this case the hacker will plant viruses, key loggers, rootkits or Trojans, all of which will relay the information they require. This could be a way to gather information regarding passwords, security protocols, improve access, etc.

The hacker will also be able to get as much unencrypted data as they can find – data that is not very well-secured because it is deemed unimportant and use this data as a way to gain entry to secured files.

Once on the premises, the hacker may be able to hide technology of their own, like a wireless access point. This enables them to continue to have access even once they have left the building.

Chapter 3

Information Gathering

This is the most crucial stage for any hacker. You need to "footprint" the system. i.e. gather as much information about it as you are able. The more you understand the system, the better the chances are that you will be able to find a vulnerability that you can exploit.

With the prolific information available online, this is made a whole lot more simple. Just go to any search engine and type keywords related to the target system. You will find pages and pages of information about it.

In fact, if you want to keep up to date on hacking techniques, you can do the same thing. Isn't it amazing exactly what information is available online?

Anyway, the main concept that I want to get across in this chapter is that how information gathering is approached is what sets a great hacker apart from a really mediocre one.

If you want to elevate your game as a hacker, this is the section that you need to pay the most attention to.

Recon

As any seasoned operative will tell you, the difference between the success and failure of a mission can hinge on the quality of information you have at your disposal. A special ops team would never go into a situation blind and neither should you.

This phase of the operation can become tedious because it means watching how things are done, when they are done and where they are done. It can be quite tedious to have to identify patterns of behavior but that is key in figuring out where the chinks in the armor lie.

Competitive Intelligence

This means the data regarding services, products, strategies and technologies in use. Instead of referring to the target system, this information is gathered from their competition.

The way the competition handles these issues can be useful for the hacker. It might give you good ideas on how to approach your target.

SpyFu

Now that you understand a bit more about how important information gathering is, we are going to look up tools that you can use to figure out what keyword the target website or its competitors are using.

The search run using this software is passive, meaning that your target is not going to know that you have been sniffing out the data.

The keywords used can give you a much better insight into the marketing strategy, target market, etc.

Using SpyFu

The system is run completely online – you don't need to download any software. Simply visit SpyFu's site and put the website address you want to search into the box provided.

A report will be generated that gives you whatever information the software was able to access. This could be keywords, links that are important, etc.

The EDGAR Database

This is necessary when you are looking for information about a large company. EDGAR provides details about companies that have been publicly listed and can be a very useful resource for you.

This allows you to see what addresses are on file with the SEC and also who the main contact people are.

Working the Database

You are going to need to find out how your company shows on the stock exchange – this is an abbreviated form of the name. For example, AMZN stands for Amazon.

You can do this by googling the company name and stock price.

Once you have that information, you need to go through to www.sec.gov and find the tab that will take you to EDGAR Filers. (It is usually on the right side of the page in a sidebar.)

Now find the tab that is labeled, "Search for Filings" and search using the abbreviated stock name of the company.

This is going to give you a fair amount of information including when and where the company was registered and who the person responsible for filing the documents was. (These are normally higher ranking individuals such as the Chief Financial Officer, etc.)

Now go through to the yellow pages on Yahoo – yp.yahoo.com and enter the name of the person who filed the documents and see if you can get more information that way. You can also repeat the search on other search engines such as Google.

To help make the search more specific, use the person's full first name and surname in quotation marks so that you get more relevant results. For example, "John Smith". This might not be specific enough because their names may come up in relation to positions they have held at previous employers as well.

Alternatively, try their name in quotation marks, followed by a plus sign and the name of the company in quotation marks to further drill down into the results. For example: "John Smith" + "Gmail".

Successful Footprinting

By now you will, at the very least, have a basic idea of who some of the key players within the organization are. You need a fuller blueprint of the whole information system to be entirely successful.

Now that you have identified key players, you need to find out where the systems server is located and who might have the access to it that you are looking for. The idea is to then hack their username and password so that you can log on as them.

This can often be done very successfully and without attracting any information by looking through the company's website. There is a lot of information available on a website – you might even find a company directory. This can be exploited to find suitable candidates to contact for social engineering tactics.

Tools That Make Footprinting Easier

Again, to list all the tools available for this task would be outside the scope of this book. What we will do instead is to go through some of the more popular and effective ones.

For now, we will look at tools that are passive in nature – this allows you to collect the data that you need without being worried that you will be detected as a hacker.

I just want to stress once again that footprinting is vital to success – it lets you know off the bat what won't work. For example, let's say that the targeted system is running on a Linux-based operating system.

If you try to attack it using tools designed for use with a Windows operating system, you are not going to get very far.

By allowing you to choose the best possible tools for the job, footprinting makes your hack more efficient and decreases the chances that your intrusion will be noticed.

The tools you might want to learn about include:

Whois: This was not originally designed for hacking but it has become a firm favorite with hackers. It can assist in finding out who the registered owner of a domain is.

All you need to do is to go to the site www.dnsstuff.com and search for the button at the bottom of the page that allows you to access the toolbox.

Access "Whois" and run a search on your target's URL.

Unless your target site owners have enabled the privacy settings on their site, you should be able to get the email address of the contact person who registered the domain, the address of the domain owner, the Technical contacts and the DNS contacts. You should also be able to find a contact phone number and when the domain name expires.

You then need to double-check as that this information is still current. This can be done by checking what it publicly available on the website and in directory listings for the company.

Even if the person listed has left, you still have an idea of what the email listing protocols for the company are.

Finding Email Addresses

See whether or not you can find any contact email addresses that use the person's name and are not a generic one. For example, admin@gmail.com would be a waste of time. However, john.smith@gmail.com is far more useful. When looking for email addresses, you don't necessarily need to look for those used by the people in charge, such as the CEO. Nine times out of ten, these are going to be difficult to identify.

People lower down on the rung, however, are not going to be as difficult to find. A sales consultant's email will be pretty easy to come across. What you are looking for here is to find out how the company's email addresses are set up and this will help you guess what the more important email addresses that you are looking for are.

Haven't been able to find any non-generic email addresses? Take the name you know, place it in quotation marks, and add + "email address". This might work for you.

If it does not, you can also try common variants of what the email address may be. So try, johnsmith@gmail.com; john.smith@gmail.com; jsmith@gmail.com; j.smith@gmail.com; smithj@gmail.com; etc.

Just search each of the varieties that you come up with and see whether or not there are matches online. (Try with and without the quotation marks – with quotation marks will help you get more relevant matches; not using quotation marks will be useful if the actual email address is very similar to the one you thought up.)

This may seem a little tedious but you would be amazed at how many documents we put our email address onto – it could be LinkedIn presentations, Pdf documents, forums, delegate lists, etc.

Packet-Tracking Tools

These tools will make it possible for you to find out what route the different data packets take within the network. This can assist you in finding where the routers and other important devices on the network are.

Packet-tracking tools are very simple tools and useful in that they present their results visually. Tools such as NeoTrace, VisualLookout and Visual Route are popular versions of this software.

If your primary goal is to track the target's emails, eMailTrackerPro and MailTracking are two popular tools that can assist you with this. If you make use of these when sending an email or replying to one, the application tracks how your original message moved along the system. You get to see where it went to and how the target system handled it.

Chapter 4

Using the Data You Gathered -

Scanning

Scanning allows you to use the information that you have collected to great effect. The more information you have, the more effective your scanning will end up being.

Scanning is an extension of the information gathering stage in that you will be collecting as much information as possible regarding the system and any other systems hosted by it or that it is hosted on.

Scanning is more than just information gathering, however. Here you are specifically looking for weaknesses that you can exploit or points of entry you can make use of.

During the scanning phase, there are basically three different ways to look for the information you want:

- **Scanning for Vulnerabilities**: This type of scanning is specifically targeted at looking for weaknesses that can be exploited to gain access to the system.

- **Scanning for Ports**: This is used to look for ports or services that may be open and so used to access a system.

- **Network Scanning**: This is used to find out what IP addresses the target system is using.

Scanning for Ports

This is done on the off-chance that there are TCP/ IP ports that are open and thus easy to use within your system.

There are many systems that run in the background on your computer. Each system will be assigned a particular port. If the computer is connected to the internet, and these ports are left open, they may offer access to the system in general.

There can be thousands of port numbers on any given computer. They are basically divided up into three different subsectors:

- **Well-Known Ports**: Range from 0 - 1023

- **Registered Ports**: Range from 1024 – 49151

- **Dynamic Ports**: Range from 49151 - 65535

As a hacker, ports that fall under the well-known category are what should interest you the most. It is good to know where the other ports fall within the ranges as well. Your software will scan the system and see whether or not there are any open ports that might suit your purposes.

If you can gain access to the system, you need to go into the Control Panel and search for "hidden files". A screen will come up where you can instruct the system to always show hidden files.

Once you have done that, run a search for C:\windows\system32\drivers\etc\services and double-click on the file. (If the system asks you what program to use to open it, try using Notepad.)

You will get a list of the various common port numbers and what applications are associated with them. It's then up to you to choose which, if any, would be suitable to exploit.

For example: 21 – FTP means that this is a File Transfer Protocol application.

Scanning the Network

This enables you to find out whether or not there are active hosts within the target system and either check how effect they are or if they are vulnerable in some way. Hosts can be identified through their IP addresses.

Using a network-scanning tool is the most effective way of finding out who the target hosts are and what address they are using.

Scanning for Vulnerabilities

This is where you are actively looking for weaknesses within the system. It is an active search and so may be detectable. You can find a number of vulnerability scanners online.

The scanner looks at the makeup of the system, focusing on the operating system and any patches or service packs. It sniffs out weakness in the defenses that can assist you in gaining entry to the system.

This is extremely important for when you want to begin your attack – by knowing what the weaknesses are, you will know how to access the information you want to steal or how to maliciously damage the whole system.

What Else You Need to Know About Scanning

Scanning can give you a shortcut when it comes to finding more information about the active hosts, but this must be weighed up against the increased likelihood that you'll get caught.

Where the system owner has taken pains to protect the system against attack, they will most likely have installed intrusion detection systems and these will normally be able to pick up attempts at scanning quite quickly.

It might also pick up that you are scanning vulnerabilities and the network because these are all active means of scanning.

The target system will then flag the activity as hostile or hacking and deploy countermeasures as applicable.

Needless to say, the hackers have also risen to the challenge and worked on scanning tools with different levels of activity. The idea is that these new tools are less likely to be recognized by the IDS. For most hackers, the end goal is to get in, get the information they want, and get out again without anyone being the wiser.

Ping Sweep Techniques

When you are ready to begin scanning, you should first start to look for systems within the network that are active. Inactive systems are useless at this stage because they do act on requests to connect or give responses to probing.

You can start off with a very simple ping sweep so that you can see whether or not the system is active. You do this on the range of IP addresses connected to the primary website.

The idea is that those systems that respond can be thought of as an active part of your target network. The problem is that this is not an extremely accurate method. It is possible that systems within the network fail to respond because they are temporarily offline, or have active anti-pinging software, etc. It is, however, a very simple method to use.

The Internet Control Message Protocol is what you will use to actually execute the commands to ping the system.

It is a versatile tool that can work well on varying kinds of devices – such as switches, routers, etc. – as long as the item in question has an IP address.

Using Windows Ping

Microsoft Windows has a ping command built into its main operating system and you can use this to effectively ping your target system.

Open the command window – you can do this by searching for "command window" and then type in "ping" followed by the site you want to ping. So, if you wanted to ping Wikihow, for example, you would type:

ping www.wikihow.com

The system will then be pinged and you will be able to see whether or not it is reacting. You can also ping using the exact IP address of the computer if you have it.

If it times out before giving you any data, then either the system is not active or it has defenses in place to block pinging attempts.

If you have the wrong address altogether, the system will tell you that.

If you do get a response it will usually be a few listings of the IP address and information about how many packets were sent and received and the turnaround time. This is an indication that the network is, in fact, active and that it will respond to pings.

Detecting Ping Sweeps on Your System

An intrusion detection or intrusion prevention system are two ways in which you can have your own system detect sweeps. The system can be programmed to contact the relevant security personnel when a sweep has been detected.

Most good firewalls and proxy servers make it impossible to reply to pings in order to ensure that hackers are not given information about whether or not the systems within the network are active.

Should pinging fail, a hacker will need to look to other techniques to scan for open ports. It can be quite frustrating for a hacker – just because the system does not respond to a ping, it doesn't mean that it is not an active system. It could just be that the firewall blocked the ping response.

For this reason, ping sweeps should be viewed as just one possible tool.

And that is also why a hacker must be a patient and determined person. Cracking a system might mean several failed attempts. The key is to learn from these attempts and try something different again.

Scanning Ports

Once you have established that there is an active computer within the system and you know its address, you can move on to scan for available ports. This again is a trial and error process – you are going to check all the ports to see which ones are open. This will often prove a lot more useful in hacking the system than ping sweeping.

Service Determination

This is another part of the scanning phase. The tools used here may be the same as the ones used to figure out whether or not there were any open ports.

As soon as you know which ports are open, you can find out which services run off those port numbers.

NMAP

This tool is quite versatile and can do a lot from actually running ping sweeps, through to identifying what ports are open, what the IP address is, and what operating system has been installed.

And you don't have to do one scan at a time – this tool can scan many different computers in one go.

The scan is also a lot more useful than a general ping. The scan will tell you precisely why you cannot access the port you want to. It will say the port is open if this is the case. If the port is simply closed, it will report that. If the attempt was foiled by a firewall or filter, you will be told that too.

Chapter 5

Password Cracking for Beginners

Password cracking might end up being a lot easier than you could ever imagine. The better you know and understand your target, the easier it will be to work out what their password is.

We will work through guessing the password to actual password cracking software in this chapter.

One, Two Three, Password

Companies and networks will have a certain protocol in place when it comes to how passwords need to be created. Each password will need to have a certain number of letters and numbers, perhaps a few capital letters, and maybe some special characters as well.

If you can establish what the password protocol for the system is, half the battle is won.

If you have done sufficient research on your target, you will be in a good position to guess what the password is.

What should be remembered is that everyone knows that they shouldn't use things that others can find out easily about them when it comes to choosing a password. But people also want things to work more easily for them. So, while they might avoid using their Christian name, they might use a nickname that they are known by, a child's name or the name of their pet.

With a little bit of judicious guessing, you might be able to guess what the password is.

Just a quick example here to illustrate the point.

I was freelancing for a client once and waiting for them to arrive to input their password so that I could input the data I was supposed to. They were late and I wanted to get on with things. I decided to see if I could guess the password.

Now this was a highly-educated man, so I realized that it wasn't going to be dead simple. I looked around the office. On the wall was his degree, complete with full names and the date he graduated.

I typed in his second name, followed by the date of graduation, and was granted access to the system. He was floored by how easy it had been.

The lesson I want you to take from this is that his password was something that he thought no one else would think of. It was, however, extremely easy to guess because I knew him well and the information was easy to find. Even if I had not known him personally, the password comprised of information that was easily accessible.

What are Strong Passwords?

Protecting your password has become a serious business. I remember in the early days when I signed up for internet banking my password consisted of my nickname and nothing else. (It has obviously changed now.)

Companies have come to realize that stronger passwords are required to ensure that they are not as easy to crack anymore.

Passwords today may include:

- Numbers

- Letters

- Special characters

- Capitalized letters

- Or any combination of the above

If you want to create a really strong password, it should:

- Consist of a minimum of eight characters in total

- Have at least one number, one letter, one special character and one capitalized letter

- If you choose a word, choose one completely at random about something that no one would ever guess at random – i.e. no pet's names, grandparent's names, etc.

- In fact, it is better to choose some randomized letters rather than a recognizable word.

- Avoid duplicating characters.

So, a password for John Smith, for example, may play out as follows:

- johnsmith – weak

- john.smith1981 – better but still too easy to guess

-

- football@54 – not bad

- RahJo465£Lf – very strong

Of course, the password that is extremely strong on this list is the most difficult to remember so you might want to try and strike a balance between something that you'll remember and switching things up a little.

Attacks to Get a Password

There are several techniques that can be used to determine what the password is. The first classification would be whether the attack will take place online or offline.

Offline Attacks

You will need to be able to get onto a device that already has details of the passwords and usernames that you are looking for. The information is then removed for later use.

Dictionary Attack: This is probably the easiest way and is one commonly used. This is also why you should use random letters and special characters instead of words in your own passwords.

A file that contains words from the dictionary is uploaded and this is then used to test the various permutations to see whether or not the guesses will work. To defeat this type of attack, use jumbled letters, numbers and special characters.

Hybrid Attack: This is put into place if the dictionary attack fails. It will run through the same words as used in the first attack but start to incorporate numbers and symbols as well. So, instead of running a word like "dictionary", it will change it to "dictionar1!" The more jumbled and the longer the password, the longer it will take the system to work through all the possible permutations.

Brute-Force Attack: This one is not fun for the hacker and can take a long time. It incorporates capitalized letters in addition to the special characters and numbers as detailed above.

This technique does take a lot more time as there are many more potential combinations but, considering current password protocols, this is the method most likely to succeed.

The way to combat this problem is to have a good detection system. This method will succeed if the hacker has enough time. Limiting the amount of time that they have before being detected is the best defense here. This means choosing longer passwords and varying the length of passwords within the system so no clear pattern in the protocol can be exploited.

Active Online Attacks

It may be simpler to try and gain access through the use of the administrator privileges. This can be done by guessing what the password is. You can do this manually if you know the target well and you might get away with it if the password is pretty weak. You could also end up being locked out of the system.

Automating Password Guesses

The use of tools can help to reduce the time needed on guessing passwords. And you can make your own scripts to help guess passwords using tools available within Windows.

Making your own scripts is simple:

Open Notepad and make your own list of passwords and usernames. A tool such as Directory Generator can help you create a list. When saving the file, call it credentials and save as a .txt file in the C drive.

Open the command window and type in the following:

C:\> FOR /F "token=1, 2*" %i in (credentials.txt)

Now see if you are able to access the hidden files within the system by using the following command:

net use \\targetIP\IPC$ %i /u: %j

Passive Online Attacks

These are safer in that the system targeted is usually not able to detect it is being attacked. These attacks are conducted online. For this method to work, the passwords are compared to a list of words in a similar manner as offline hacks. The difference here is that the password is confirmed through accessing the user verification process.

This can be a little trickier because you need a program to work around the encryption of the user verification systems. (This encryption is in place to make hacking more difficult.)

A program such as Man-In-The-Middle is often used to affect these passive attacks.

The hacker essentially hijacks the request for authentication sent legitimately, extracts the information they want, and then delivers it to the sever.

This is accomplished by implanting a sniffer – a program that is able to both monitor requests between users and servers and a program that is able to capture passwords. The sniffer is implanted between the target system and the server to facilitate the hijacking of legitimate requests.

An alternative is to use a replay attack. In this case, you don't actually even need to know what the password is. You capture data in the same way on its way to the server but instead of using the password, authentication packets that will work in future will be sent.

Cracking Passwords Manually

There are going to be times when you will need to figure out the password without help from automated programs. This is harder, but if you follow the following steps, you should make progress:

- See if you can find an account that is authorized on the system – such as an administrator or username if you can find one.

- Start working out what passwords would fit the password protocols of the site.

- List these in order of those with the highest possibility of success to those with the least.

- Now you just need to plug in each potential password until you find one that fits. (Or write a script that does it for you.)

Manual cracking should really be a last resort – it is extremely time-consuming and there is a very high risk that you will be blocked from the system for trying the password too many times. Unless you have a pretty good idea of what the password is, this method has limited success.

Tools for Cracking Passwords

Here are some tools that you might want to add to your hacking arsenal:

- **Legion**: You will use this if you want help guessing the password. It works with systems that run in NetBIOS. It will look through various ranges of IP addresses and it also makes a dictionary hacking tool available to you.

- **NTInfoScan**: If you are trying to hack an NT4.0 device, this is the tool for you. It scans the target for issues with the security that can be exploited.

-

- **LophtCrack**: This is a password recovery tool and can launch attacks of various natures so that even the toughest passwords can be cracked. It might be difficult to get your hands on a copy though. If you cannot find it, LC5 is a good alternative.

- **John the Ripper**: This works on Unix and NT systems. It is not always effective as it does not pick up differences in letter cases.

Chapter 6

Applications to Gain Entry to

Systems

Here we are going to discuss the two primary ways that hackers use to get access to your system.

Trojans and Backdoors

These are both examples of malware. (Malware or malicious software is designed to be implanted in your system with the intent of gathering information or making it easier to access the system – without your consent.) Both types of malware operate in a similar manner.

Backdoors

As the name implies, this is something that makes accessing the system at a future time possible. The backdoor may be hidden in with other software and, when done right, be undetectable.

Secrecy is the main aim when it comes to backdoor access – you want to be able to access the system as and when you please and so you should create as little flaggable activity as possible.

Backdoors are often made part of freeware offerings online. When you install the freeware, the backdoor is installed at the same time. If you are a hacker, getting someone to use a new program that seems harmless is an excellent way to introduce the backdoor.

The malware will often be disguised amongst the other files and hackers use generic names for them that won't raise flags. So, if you are looking for backdoor programs on your system, look for filenames that seem innocuous, files that wouldn't ordinarily arouse suspicion.

To be effective as a hacker, you need to practice efficiency of movement – minimize the changes that you make and make as little impact on the activity logs as you can. This will help you further avoid detection.

Remote Access Trojans

These can be very difficult to detect. The system owner is able to use the system as normal while the program is running in the background. The system then opens a network port so that the hacker has access.

This kind of Trojan interacts directly with the target system's operating system and may have separate files for what the servers sees and what the user sees. The former file is placed onto the actual computer while the other file can be used on the network to effect change.

These are difficult to detect but you can find them if you look out for them carefully. Look for unusual actions by the computer – system resources being used when the system is idling or pop-ups that seem to appear out of nowhere.

Trojans

This is a blanket term to describe a range of different malware. It's based on the story of the Trojan Horse – the Greeks snuck into the city of Troy disguised within the belly of a giant horse that they'd built. The Trojans brought the horse into the city because they didn't know that the Trojans were hiding inside and so lost the war.

Trojans are designed to look harmless or even to look helpful. You may find that there are features of the program that are quite useful for you. This is to encourage you to keep the program active. In fact, freeware is one of the biggest vehicles for Trojans.

In reality, though, their purpose is a more insidious one. Once installed, they allow the hacker full access to your network.

The Trojan will, at best, steal data held on your computer and transmit it to the hacker. If the hacker is more malicious, the Trojan could end up slowing down your system. If they want to create complete mayhem, a Trojan can also be designed to destroy the data on the infected computer or network.

Trojans can be programmed to take over control of how the system operates and how well you are able to use it. They are excellent information gathering tools and can be programmed with a key logger. They allow the hacker to view your data and to run whatever commands they like. Trojans can also be designed to infect other computers within the network or computers that have been emailed by yours.

Trojans can be transmitted in a number of ways – through an attachment to an email or instant message; through an online download, through a manual download from a disk or thumb drive or through file sharing protocols.

Types of Trojans

The type of Trojan will depend on what the aim of the hacker is.

- **Proxy**: These Trojans are designed to allow an attack on a different network or to open up another way to attack a system.

- **DOS**: These are popular when it comes to denying an authorized user access to a system.

- **Destructive**: The aim here is to damage the system – it will delete data or corrupt it.

- **FTP**: These enable the creation of servers that are able to place files into the target network.

- **Security Disabler**: Needless to say, antivirus programs can cause headaches for hackers. These Trojans render them harmless.

Hackers Go-To Trojans

As you are developing as a hacker, you will find out what Trojans work best with your method. Here are some that you can look into to start off with:

- TROJ_QAZ: This is linked into the Notepad app within Windows. It is an executable file that runs as soon as Notepad is launched. Hackers use this as a backdoor to enable them access to the system and gain control over it.

- Netcat: This makes use of commandline interface to open ports within the target system. This enables the hacker to use those ports to access the network. Netcat is easy to find online.

- Tini: This works with the Windows operating system and is quite a small program. It allows the hacker to command the target system through the 7777 port.

Chapter 7

Wireless Hacking

Of course, part of the thrill of being a hacker is in being able to connect to a wireless network. It opens up such a wide range of possibilities to be able to connect wirelessly. But what if your own network is down or what if you want to get free wi-fi?

I am not going to get into an ethical discussion on whether or not you should be hacking someone else's wi-fi network. As a hacker, though, it is a skill that you want to learn.

When it comes to a wireless network, there are a couple of security issues that you can make work to your advantage – bad configuration or bad encryption. If the network is not adequately protected with the right security protocols and a strong password, it will be much easier to hack.

If you want to hack the network, you'll need to crack the wireless password for it. Here are some tools that you can do to get this right:

Aircrack

This is a tool that is extremely popular. It works by gathering different packets of data. When it has a sufficient number of packets, it begins working out what the password is.

If you are a complete beginner, you can make use of the tutorial that the company offers. It will walk you through the process step by step. This tool is highly popular because it is highly effective.

You are, however, going to need some knowledge of Linux. That said, it is worth mastering this tool because it is extremely effective when used properly.

Find it at: http://www.aircrack-ng.org/

AirSnort

Yet another tool that is both popular and free. It can be used on both Windows and Linux. The company no longer provides support or updates but you can still find the program online. It works in much the same way that Aircrack does but is quite a bit simpler to operate.

Find it at: http://sourceforge.net/projects/airsnort/

Cain & Able

This tool makes use of a brute force attack to determine what the passwords within a system are. It will help to sniff out network keys for you as well. This is a really good tool for a beginner to use.

Find it at: http://www.oxid.it/cain.html

NetStumbler

This will help you to find wireless access ports that are open. It can be downloaded for free and works on Windows systems.

It is simple to use but makes use of active collection techniques, including active probes and this makes it easy to detect.

The company that developed it no longer runs updates and this can make it glitchy with newer versions of Windows.

Find it at: http://www.stumbler.net/

These are just a few of the programs available out there to help you crack passwords. I would strongly suggest that you read up more on the subject as there are new programs and countermeasures being developed daily.

In the game of hacking, a hacker who doesn't keep up is soon made obsolete.

Conclusion

Wow, I guess that's about all I have to say. I hope that you understand the process of hacking a bit better now and I do hope that you are excited about putting the skills you have learned to practice.

Whether you just want to have a bit of fun by hacking systems to see if you can, or you want to do this as a way of living, I wish you luck.

I do want to leave you with one small word of warning, though. Unless you have the system owner's particular permission to hack the system, doing so is highly illegal. The use of hacking software can also be illegal in some countries and so I urge you to do a little research before you use any of the software or methods dealt with in this book.

I also urge you to consider who you are hacking carefully. If you are looking to create a little bit of mischief, hacking the U.S. Department of Defense, for example, is not a good idea! If you are successful and are caught, you could find yourself in deep trouble legally and could be imprisoned.

Have fun but be sensible!

Book Two Starts Here

Hacking

The Complete Beginner's Guide To Computer

Hacking: More On How To Hack Networks &

Computer Systems, Information Gathering,

Password Cracking, System Entry & Wireless

Hacking

Jack Jones

Table of Contents

Chapter 7: Countermeasures

Detecting Attacks

Detecting an Intrusion

Countermeasures and the Hacker

How to Stay Hidden as a Hacker

The Tools You Will Need

Altering the Log Files

Using Meterpreter to Clear the Event Logs

Clearing the Event Logs in a Machine Running Windows

Clearing Up Event Logs on a Machine Running Linux

Deleting your Command History

Destroy Your History File

Making the Attack Seem Normal

Chapter 8: A Little About Cryptography

Encryption and the Net

Chapter 9: Putting Your New Skills to Use

A Keylogger

Denial of Service

Waterhole attacks

Eavesdropping

Phishing

Virus, Trojan etc.

Spyware

Malware

Clickjacking Attacks

Introduction

Say the word "hacker" and most people conjure up pictures of some misfit loner who never follows the rules and can access even the most sensitive information with a few clicks on the keyboard. Many people have two ideas of what hackers are – either criminals out to steal their private information or people who just want to cause chaos.

The truth is somewhat different. While there are hackers out there who do use their skills to steal information or to cause chaos, that is not what hacking is really about. Hacking is about testing systems with the intent of finding weaknesses. It's more about problem solving and, when used within the law, can be an extremely useful security exercise.

Hacking is a modern-day artform and, as such, is generally misunderstood. Dedicated hackers are constantly working on refining their skills and looking for ways to improve the efficiency of systems. Most hackers believe that information should be freely available and buck against a system that gets in the way of this.

The so-called Hacker Ethic entails valuing logic as its own type of art form; promoting the free access to information and overcoming the boundaries of the conventional systems. In some cases, this is going to entail activities that are, by their nature, somewhat illegal, but nonetheless well-intentioned intentions.

So, whilst hacking into a company's system is illegal, if you are doing it to expose weaknesses for them, you are working with good intentions. It allows them to improve the system and make it less prone to future attacks.

And, yes, as with anything else in like there are hackers that are not nearly as ethical. Hackers who do aim to cause mayhem in systems and steal information for their own benefit. Hackers who take over systems and then make the owners pay to regain control. This book is not intended for hackers like that.

This book is aimed at the ethical hacker – a hacker that embraces what hacking was originally about. In this book, we assume that you already have some idea of the basics of hacking, such as gathering information, etc.

We will go into hacking techniques in more detail so that you can start to apply them and start to gain experience for yourself. The goal of this book is to expand on the basics and to inspire you to start looking at ways to improve the current techniques available or even to start developing your own.

The aim of this book is to get you excited about hacking again and to help you to develop your own interpretation of the art of hacking.

reader. Under no circumstances will any legal responsibility or blame be held against the publisher for any reparation, damages, or monetary loss due to the information herein, either directly or indirectly.

Respective authors own all copyrights not held by the publisher.

The information herein is offered for informational purposes solely, and is universal as so. The presentation of the information is without contract or any type of guarantee assurance.

The trademarks that are used are without any consent, and the publication of the trademark is without permission or backing by the trademark owner. All trademarks and brands within this book are for clarifying purposes only and are the owned by the owners themselves, not affiliated with this document.

Chapter 1

Programming for Hackers

There are basically two broad categories when it comes to hackers – those who write their own code and those who exploit an existing code. In both cases, the results are different but the basic problem-solving techniques are very similar.

Those who exploit code are better able to do so if they understand some programming. Those who write their own code are better able to do so if they understand the art of exploitation. As a result, you will find that most hackers are able to use either system.

Program Exploits

Program exploits usually work by exploiting weaknesses in the system and rules and using them to bypass security in a manner the original programmer did not intend.

Programming Hacks

Programming hacks are pretty similar because they also work using the system rules in a way that was unintended but the end goal tends to be greater efficiency or a pared down version of the source code instead of just an out and out compromise of security.

If you are a hacker, you could put yourself to work in working on more elegant solutions for software that a company uses. In the development phase of most software, functionality is more importance than elegance or pared down code.

The focus is on creating code that works in as short a time as possible. With computer processing power rising all the time, it is no longer necessary to spend extra time making the code a little bit faster or more efficient.

What is Programming?

A computer is not able to think for itself. It must be told what to do step by step. Programmers lay out every step that the computer must take in a logical order so that a particular function can be achieved.

It is essentially like a recipe that you use to cook a meal except that the language used must be one the computer will understand. And this is where it becomes more difficult for your average person.

Writing code can be difficult and can be tedious. If you don't leave a space where you are supposed to or if you make a simple spelling mistake, your code is not going to work well, if at all. If you leave out one step or even a single character, the system will not be able to understand what you want and the program will not work as it should.

There are many different types of programming languages out there such as Java, C++, etc. The type you use will depend on which works best for you and what your system requirements are.

Translating the Code So the Computer Can Read It

Your computer reads information as binary numbers – a series of ones and zeroes. This is known as machine code. You will write the code in the programming language of your choice. This is programming code.

You then need to convert the programming code into machine code. You could do this manually if you wanted to but it is really difficult to do.

What you need to do is to get a compiler. This is software that will convert high-level programming language, like C++ into machine code. The compiler can convert the code into machine language for various different architectures.

The advantage of using a high-level language is that it is a lot easier for humans to read. You can write out the instructions in something that resembles English instead of machine code. You do, however, need to be careful to follow the rules for the programming language or the compiler is not going to be able to do its job.

Chapter 2

Important Programming Concepts

Dealing in full with programming is beyond the scope of this book. What we will do instead is to go over the most important concepts.

Pseudo-Code

Pseudo-code is another type of language used by programmers. All it really is, is English that has been written in a similar fashion to programming language.

It is not readable by computers or compilers and may be used as a first step when writing out your code.

It helps you to set out the basic instructions and structure and this can then be converted into a high-level programming language. It is like a basic road-map before you move onto the programming language.

Control Structures

If you didn't have control structures in place, your program would be nothing more than a set of instructions that the computer executes one after another. When you need something very simple done, that's not a problem.

For more complex programming needs, control structures need to be put in place. Let's say, for example, that you need to write a program for when to activate a motion-sensitive light.

This is not a simple program. You would need to alter how the execution of the program flows. In our example, you would need to put in something like, "If the motion sensor is activated, the light must be switched on." This would change the flow of instructions.

If-Then-Else

You need to consider all possibilities when programing something. You will have to tell the computer how to react to different variables it encounters.

Take the motion sensor light example again. You could add an instruction that if the beam is broken for 3 seconds, the light must be activated.

So, you would write a code in this kind of format:

If (whatever the condition is) then

{whatever you want the computer to do should the condition be met;

} Else

{whatever you want the computer to do should the condition not be met.}

This is the pseudo-code we were talking about earlier. You would need to convert it into the programming language you are using. Setting it out in pseudo-code first is an extra step but it makes it easier to ensure that you have a logical flow worked out and exactly what each step entails. From there on, it is easy enough to convert it.

While/Until Loops

The while control structure is a basic concept in programming and is a loop of sorts. There will be many times when you need the same set of instructions to be executed repeatedly.

Looping enables you to do this but does mean that you need to be specific about when the loop starts and stops. If you don't input this information, the loop will be repeated ad infinitum.

The while loop sets out sets out the conditions that must prevail for the loop to be repeated. The until loop performs a similar function except that it instructions the computer to repeat the loop until a specific condition has been reached.

For Loops

Alternatively, you can program a set number or repetitions. So, for example, you could tell the light to stay on after the motion sensor has been activated for 5 minutes.

Variables

When you added the five-minute timing into the loop, what you were doing is introducing a variable. Variables can be changeable. If the variable is not changeable, it is called a constant.

So, in the light example, the time the light stayed on for was a variable. The brightness of the light, however, would be a concept.

In most programming languages, you have to declare what the variables are and what type they are before you can use them. It is like listing all the ingredients necessary for a recipe – you need to know what all of these are before you start cooking.

The variables will all be stored somewhere in the computer's memory. The declarations that you made upfront about what the variables are make it possible for the computer to make more efficient use of these.

Comparison Operators

You will need to write in comparison operators when you are using conditional statements such as the "If/ Then/ Else" control structures.

For example, you may need to say something like, if B < 10, then. The "<" symbol is the comparison operator.

Functions

Functions are a set of instructions that has been grouped into a subprogram. This is a basic shortcut when you need to repeat that same set of instructions a few times. You start out by declaring what the function is and name it. From then on, you only need to write in the function name instead of having to write out the instructions all over again.

Understanding how programming works and being able to write your own programs is essential to being a great hacker. Without a basic knowledge of programming, you will never be able to find weaknesses in the system or write exploits or fixes for them.

Chapter 3

Why You Need to Install Linux

For most hackers, Linux is the go-to operating system. It is an opensource operating system that offers the user pretty much complete control. You can use it in place of Microsoft Word and users tend to prefer it because they can control what they want to control – not just what Microsoft thinks they should control.

Many of the Distros for Linux can be downloaded for free. Ubuntu is one of the most common of these. Some of the Linux OS such Kali Linux have been developed especially for finding security holes and pen testing. Kali Linux is also a popular choice amongst hackers.

Because Linux is opensource, you are free to copy it, edit it and distribute any of the components legally. There is no concern about copyright infringement or special terms. You can dig right in and see how it works and access the source code. If you are planning on writing code for hacking with, this is an essential component.

There are many developer forums available if you need help with fixing some kind of bug. It is a very friendly community with developers all around the world willing to assist you.

The system is a lot lighter than Windows. It takes up less room on your system and does draw as heavily on your system resources. You can run it alongside another OS very easily, without worrying about draining resources.

There is a widespread belief out there that Linux is a difficult program to master and that you need some serious programming or hacking skills to be able to use it. This is the opposite of what most users say, though. Most users find it a lot easier to use than Windows.

Most importantly for the hacker, though, is that most hacking tools are written for Linux. It is believed that only around 10% of hacking tools are written for other operating systems.

Kali Linux is Linux's most advanced penetration testing tool.

Chapter 4

Exploitation

Exploitation of computer programs can be considered a staple. In the first two chapters, we explored how computer programs are simply a set of rules set up in a logical fashion that explain to the computer how it must behave.

If you understand how programming works, you can more easily find exploits that enable you to insert your own instructions, even when there are security measures in place.

It can be difficult to build a program from the ground up – the programmer has to write pages and pages of code. It is very easy to make a mistake and leave a small hole in the security of the program that a hacker is able to exploit.

Some errors are pretty easy to find and make use of, others require a certain amount of finesse. Once you have managed to insert your code, the computer will run the program in the way it always done, except with your code being inserted.

The program will not be able to distinguish between code that is added legitimately and code added by a hacker. It will only do what its program says it should. In addition, programmers might not always write exactly what they mean.

Even a small mistake here can make the system more vulnerable. Look at it this way. Say you were building a fence 100-feet long, spacing the posts at 10 feet apart. How many posts would you need in total. You'd think that 10 would be the logical answer, wouldn't you?

You'd be wrong – you actually also need a post at the starting point of the fence so you need 11 in total. It seems like a silly little error when you think about it but it would end up changing the whole fence. Instead of having a fence that's a 100-feet long, your fence would be 90 feet because you counted the spaces instead of the number of poles.

Logically speaking, 10 poles feels right - 100 divided by 10 is 10. In programming, it is easy to make this kind of error and, to make things more difficult, even harder to pick it up.

This works out well for the hacker because it gives you an avenue to exploit. Let's say, for example, that the programmer enters a statement like:

If less than 5, shut the system down. If more than 5, keep the system running.

Great, all your bases are covered, aren't they? What happens if the reading is 5 though?

The more complex the program, the more likelihood there is that errors like this could creep in. Newly released programs may be more vulnerable because programming errors have not been found yet. Newly expanded programs may be vulnerable for the same reason.

You can find a number of hacking programs designed to sniff out vulnerabilities like this one.

Generalized Exploit Techniques

Taking advantage of errors might mean approaching the subject from another angle. Part of the art of hacking is to take advantage of vulnerabilities in ways that are not so readily apparent.

Coding mistakes are fairly common but not always that easy to find. They may seem to have little impact on the program and the way it operates. They can also be found in a number of different areas of the code.

To speed up finding these errors, general exploit techniques are very useful. The aim of the exploit techniques is to gain control over the execution of tasks and insert your own piece of code so that the computer does what you want it to do.

Buffer Overflow Vulnerabilities

This is an old hack but it can work very well. It can be present in many different types of software, all the way from your operating system to applications that are loaded. It is generally as a result of sloppy programming and possibly the lack of proper input validation.

What Does Buffer Overflow Mean?

This occurs when a program that is running tries to write data outside of the area or memory buffer that the data was meant to be stored on. To understand a bit more about this, you need to understand what a memory buffer is. It is basically an area within the RAM of the computer that is used to store data on a temporary basis.

The problem occurs when the data recorded to the buffer is more than what was initially expected. So, let's say, for example, 8 bytes of data has been allocated to a specific memory buffer. If the program requires that 10 bytes of data be written, the data "spills" over into the next available store of memory.

It is usually as the result of poor planning on the part of the programmer.

What is Going to Happen?

Problems occur when the data overwrites other, critical program data. The program could lose stability, return corrupt data or crash.

Buffer overflows are a serious security risk because they can allow the hacker to take control of the system, run malicious commands, and enable the execution of arbitrary code.

Privilege Escalation and Arbitrary Code Execution

The hacker can use the buffer overflow vulnerability to add malicious data to the memory and so take over the running of the program. Arbitrary code execution is a process whereby the hacker injects code into the buffer and causes it to be executed.

The hacker with then be able to escalate their own privileges. (In order to do this, you need to be able to execute the code in a program that has full system privileges or administrator privileges.)

When the malicious code is run under the program, it will also run with full administrator privileges

Denial of Service (DoS)

It will not always be possible to be able to achieve arbitrary code execution but you might be able to run denial of service attacks. These simply crash the system being attacked but are not limited to computer systems. Anything that has an operating system can also be hacked and subject to the DoS attacks.

Crashing the system may not seem like a big deal, but it can be debilitating for the system being subjected to the attack, especially as they can cause the system to reboot every few minutes.

Compiling Exploits for Windows Systems Using Kali Linux

The truth is that you will need to develop exploits for Windows machines – Windows is, after all the company that holds the lion's share when it comes to market share. You are bound to encounter a lot more Windows-run systems than others.

Most of the penetration testers are compiled using Linux-operated distributions. In order to make the change over, you need to be able to compile exploits for Windows within your Linux-based operating system.

Mingw-w64

You need a compiler like Mingw-w64. This is also free, open source software and has been designed to create applications for Windows.

Unless you have a more up to date version than Kali Linux 2016.2, you will need to install mingw-w64 yourself.

Once you have installed the software, you are ready to start compiling your exploit. You need to start by downloading the exploit you need from the Exploit Database. Then you can run the exploit through your compiler to convert it to something that will work with a Windows system.

Finding Exploits Within the Exploit Database

Exploits need to be written for the specific service, application or operating system vulnerability. There is, unfortunately, no one skeleton key for all systems. If you want some help in this area, the Exploit Database is a valuable Resource.

It has been developed by the same people who came up with Kali Linux and BackTrack. The idea was to create a complete database of exploits that can be referred to as needed. The exploits are sorted by type, port, language, platform, etc. to make it easier for users to find the exploit that they are looking for.

Find the one most suitable for the system that you are targeting and then simply copy it and drop it into Kali so you can launch your attack. The steps to follow are as follows:

- **Start Kali and Get Your Browser Up and Running**: Kali's default browser is Iceweasel but you can use any browser that you like. (You can also access the database from any other operating system that you may be running.) Using the default browser has a big advantage because it has a short-cut to Exploit-db built into it. If using the default browser, all you have to do is click on the short cut. Alternatively, run a search for "Exploit Database" in the browser you choose.

- **Search for the Exploit**: Find the "Search" box in the menu bar on the site. This will enable you to type in the specific system that you want to exploit. The search function is useful because there are over 39 000 exploits listed on the system. If you know a lot about the system you are attacking, you can choose the "More Options" area of the "Search" function. This will let you input the Author, Platform, Language, Type, Port. You can also search using the "Free Text Search" or a description of the exploit. The OSVDB option should be completed if you know there is an actual, numbered vulnerability to be taken advantage of. You can further drill the search results down according to whether or not they are verified, include DoS exploits, etc.

- **To Open up an Exploit**: You can simply click on the search result that seems best suited for your purposes. Doing so will bring up the exploit itself, information about it and the code you need.

- **Using Kali's Built-In Link**: Because Kali was developed by the same folks that developed the Exploit Database, it already has some of those exploits built into it. To see what is there, open "Applications" and then select "Kali Linux". After that look for "Exploitation Tools" and then bring up the "Exploit Database".

The Exploit Database contains a lot more information besides exploits. There are several other hacks listed and also a range of tutorials about hacking or securing systems. You can use the code as is or customize it to suit your requirements more closely.

Exploit Compilation Errors

Once you have started compiling the different exploits to suit a different operating system or architecture, there are a range of errors that you may encounter. Compiling software relies on a range of different variables, and a mistake in any of these can cause compiling errors. Some are simple and fixed easily. Others are harder to work with.

You will also need to make the distinction between fatal errors and warnings. The former must be fixed and will make the compilation unworkable. The latter might not be as serious and, even if unrepaired, will not prevent the exploit working properly.

If you do get an error message at this stage, the best thing to do is to read through it and see if you can make sense of it. If you are not sure of the fix, you can always search online for a solution. A lot of people may have experienced the same problem before you did.

Chapter 5

Penetration Testing

Penetration Testing (pen testing) is the process of "attacking" a computer system, etc. with the aim of finding vulnerabilities that could be exploited by an attacker.

The testing can be done by you personally or through the use of specialized software – like Kali Linux. In either event, you are going to go to act and think like a hacker would. You will start out by running reconnaissance on your target, gathering as much useful information as possible. You will then try to find vulnerabilities and hack the system – either using a virtual copy or the real thing. Then you compile your report.

The primary aim when it comes to pen testing is to establish whether or not there are weaknesses that can be exploited. It can also be branched out to include a check on the compliance in terms of the company's security policy; how aware the employees are of security; and how well the company is able to identify and correctly respond to a breach in online security.

The primary aim with these tests is to find out how secure a system is – it is a technique that is primarily associated with ethical hackers. It is also employed by unethical hackers, though.

Strategies that pen testers might use are:

- **Targeted Testing**: This is usually when the pen testing team and the company's IT department work together. In this so-called "light-turned-on" technique, all parties are aware of the test and can see what is going on.

- **External testing**: With this technique, the company's servers/ devices that are visible to the web are attacked. This include DNS, web servers, firewalls and e-mail servers. The aim here is to see whether or not you can gain access and how much further you are able to go before being stopped.

- **Internal Testing**: In this kind of test, the attack comes from the inside using the credentials of an employee with normal access.

The idea here is to see what kind of damage could be inflicted by an unhappy employee.

- **Blind Testing**: This is closer to what would actually happen in the real world. In this case, the hacker running the test would be given only the very basic information – such as the company name. The hacker then needs to find all the relevant information that is needed for the hack for themselves.

- **Double Blind Testing**: This is another step beyond the blind test and even closer to what would happen in the real world. Here only a limited number of people within the organization are aware that the system is being tested. This is the most useful type of pen testing to check the security of the organization as a whole. It is the closest thing to what a malicious hacker would do.

A Career as a Penetration Tester

You might wonder what possible applications ethical hacking could have. After all, you are not stealing information or trying to destroy data. Isn't that what most hackers do?

The truth is that an ethical hacker can make a very good living for themselves legally, through hiring themselves out to companies that want their systems tested.

To start off with, it pays to decide upfront what type of pen testing you want to start doing. Are you going to work on applications or networks? Or perhaps you will work on building relationships with the employees of the organization to get the information from them. You need to decide where your strengths lie and work on building a career accordingly.

Let's say, for example, you have a background in application testing. That would give you a great grounding for checking for security vulnerabilities in applications. There is a lot of scope for someone who is able to hack applications and who can then suggest ways to fix any issues encountered.

According to research conducted by White Hat Security recently, the number of application testers compared to the number of applications is woefully inadequate. It was found that even if the numbers of application testers were increased tenfold, they could only test about 2% of the more important of the web apps we have today. And, considering how the app market has exploded, this situation is bound to get worse.

You have two choices if you want to make this your new career – you need either the correct certifications or the correct background. In this game, experience definitely counts for more so if you have been an application tester, for example, for the last 10 years, you don't really need to have formal qualifications.

If you are starting out from scratch, you will need to get certified or have some formal education in the topic to convince people that you know what you are doing.

Penetration Testing 101 - Hacking XP

The best way to see how penetration testing works is to actually practice doing it.

Now, I realize that XP is quite an old version of Windows but it is a good way to get your toes in the water and is much easier to hack than Windows 7 and up. In order to practice, it is best to set up a virtual machine to attack rather than attacking someone's actual computer.

You are going to need:

- **VMWare Tools**: These allow you to run a Kali Linux system and an unpatched virtual computer on the same machine.

- **A virtual machine**: This is what you will attack – there is nothing illegal about doing it this way.

- **Kali Linux**: We are going to use this for its range of pen testing tools.

- **Windows XP**: This needs to be installed on your virtual machine. Unfortunately, this you might need to buy. Try checking with friends and family who might have the discs but have upgraded to a newer version of Windows. You need a version that hasn't been patched.

Once you have everything together, you can get started.

The Metasploit Framework

We need this in order to do our hacks. How you start up the framework is going to depend on how new your version of Kali Linux is. Try running these commands – if they work, it means you have an older version of Kali Linux and must include these commands each time. If they bring up error messages, you can just leave them out completely.

If you have an older version, you will need to start by using the command "service postgresql start" in order to launch PostgreSQL.

When that is running, you then need to launch your Metasploit service. When doing this for the very first time, it will take a little longer because it needs to create databases.

Once that is running, you type in the command service Metasploit start and, once that is running, you are ready to start. It is after this point that both old and new versions of Kali Linux work the same way.

To get the framework started, you must type in "msfconsole".

The next step is to actually detect your target machine. This will require doing a port scan.

Run a Port Scan

This is where Metasploit comes into its own. It has a brilliant function for port scanning called the auxiliary scanner. To run the scan, you need to type in "use auxiliary/scanner/portscan/tcp".

Follow this by typing in "show options".

To make this easier, you will want to reduce the number of ports scanned by using the "set ports" command. You can append the number of ports to scan after this. Perhaps 1-250 or 1-450. This will reduce the time it takes the software to scan the ports.

Next you need to input the IP address of the target. This is the difficult part when it comes to hacking a remote computer. On your virtual XP run computer, you can check this out by running the "ipconfig" command.

The IP address you are given is what you will need to use in the RHOSTS command in Kali.

You type in the command "set RHOSTS" and a space and then append the IP address.

All you need to do is to now type in the command "run".

The program will scan the target computer and alert you to ports that are open or that can be attacked. If you are using a patched version of XP, you won't see any results here.

If this is the case for you, you can try to shut down the firewall on XP and do the scan again. This time you should find open ports.

Port Scanning in the Real World

If you were actually doing this in the real world, you would have to do a lot of research to find out what the IP address, operating system and open ports are in the system you are targeting. If you don't have this information, you can use the Nmap port scanner instead.

Locating Exploits

Now you need to establish which exploits, if any, will work on the particular operating system of our target. (You can check up on the Exploit Database for suitable exploits.)

If you haven't already backed out of the scanner, do so now.

Let us say that you have decided to use the dcom exploit. (One that is well-known for Windows).

You then need to type in the command that allows you to use the exploit. Do so by typing in "use exploit/windows/dcerpc/ms03_26_dcom".

You should now have the IP address of your target so set that as the RHOSTS as we did before.

Next type in the command "set" followed by a space and then "PAYLOAD", again followed by a space with windows/shell_bind_tcp appended to the end of it. Follow this up with the "exploit" command.

And just like that, you have gained access to your target. You can now access an open shell in the system that has complete admin privileges. From there, you can do whatever you like.

Chapter 6

Networking

The great technical advances we as a species have made can be ascribed to our ability to communicate. Because we have found a way to communicate with one another, we can collaborate, share our experience, and learn from others.

The same can be said when it comes to computers and computer programs. Programs can become a good deal more powerful when they are able to communicate with one another through a network. This can be in the form of a local area network where computers are connected within a specific organization or where computers are connected online. A web browser is not powerful because of the software itself but rather because it is able to open lines of communication with a number of different webservers.

Networking is something that all of us do, usually without even really knowing about it. A lot of the applications that we use on a day to day basis are reliant on networking in order to work properly. The web, your instant messages and your email all work through networking.

The applications each come with they own set of network protocols but all of these use the same transport methods across the networks. As a hacker, it is the vulnerabilities in these protocols that can be taken advantage of.

The OSI Model

For computers to be able to communicate with one another, they must both use the same language. The OSI model explains how this language is structured. The model gives standards and norms that enable the hardware, like your router, to maintain focus on only the communication aspect that is applicable to them. They will ignore everything else.

The model can be categorized as having several layers when it comes to communication. Each component along the way will focus on sending its data along its allocated layer and ignore the rest. This makes the system more efficient. For example, the router can pass the data through in the lower tiers of the system without the need to run it through the data encapsulation that is used when running applications and positioned in the higher tiers.

There are seven layers in total:

- **Physical Layer**: This layer is meant for the actual physical connection that exists between Point A and Point B. This is the lowest level and its main function is to transfer raw bit streams. It is here that bit-stream communications are maintained, activated and deactivated.

- **Data-Link Layer**: It is here that data transfer actually takes place. Unlike the former layer, that is only able to send the raw bits, high-level functions are also performed in this layer. These include flow control and the correction of errors. Here the procedures for deactivating, maintaining and activating data-link connections are provided.

- **Network Layer**: You should consider this the middle ground. The main function here is to pass data from the lower to higher layers and back. It is here that routing and addressing is provided.

- **Transport Layer**: It is here that the data is transparently transferred from one system to another. This layer is all about data communication that is reliable. This frees the higher layers of worrying whether the transmission of the data is cost-effective or reliable.

- **Session Layer**: It is here where the connection between one network application and another are established and maintained.

- **Presentation Layer**: It is here that the data is presented to the applications in a manner that enables them to understand it. This layer can compress data and encrypt it.

- **Application Layer**: In this layer, the focus is on keeping a handle on what the application requires.

The data that is moved through each of these layers is sent in little pieces known as packets. The packet in each case has implementations of the protocol layers. The data starts at the Application layer and then the presentation layer is wrapper over it, and so on until all the layers have been wrapped. This is what is known as encapsulation.

Every layer that has been wrapped has its own header and body. The header sets out what protocol information the layer requires. The body gives the data that is to be used in that layer. Each successive layer encapsulates the previous one entirely. It is like and onion – peel off one layer and there is another directly beneath it until you get back to the starting point again.

Chapter 7

Countermeasures

When it comes to hacking, it is natural that the system evolves. The more a particular hack is used, the more countermeasures will be developed in defense against it. The hackers then look for ways around the countermeasures and so on and so forth.

Whilst being attacked is not a pleasant experience, it should be seen as useful because it highlights weaknesses that are in the system and you are forced to come up with a suitable response.

This is where the ethical hacker can really be of service to their community. They could perhaps install a worm that doesn't do much in the way of damage in order to make sure that companies fix the problem and start to develop countermeasures.

Much like a vaccination, this minor infection will help protect against a devastating, malicious attack at a later stage. If nothing goes wrong in this manner, the company that developed the software or application is unlikely to look for security fixes itself and that puts everyone at risk.

That being said, a more proactive approach will always be the better option. The development of countermeasures can help to either stop an attack in its tracks or to reduce the impact of the attack so minimal damage is done.

Countermeasures come in a range of forms – from policies the company has regarding security procedures, a physical product or program or an administrator to monitor the system.

There are two broad categories when it comes to countermeasures – there are those that are designed to detect attacks and those that work to protect vulnerabilities. In an ideal world, both sets should be employed for the best level of protection.

Detecting Attacks

The aim here is to detect that an intrusion has occurred and to deal with it. This could be as simple as someone monitoring the logs or an automated program that is designed to find anomalies. The aim then is to cut off the attack as soon as possible and repair any damage done.

Detecting attacks is valuable even if you cannot do much about them at first because it lets you know that something has to be dealt with. The sooner you are able to find an attack, the sooner you can start working to nullify it.

Malicious hackers that are able to gain access to the system with the intent of stealing information will usually not just make one attack and then leave you alone. They will come back and exploit the weakness as often as they like so leaks like this must be plugged sooner rather than later.

The further along the attack is, the more difficult it might become to cut it off because the hacker would have had access to a lot more systems.

Detecting an Intrusion

If you are looking for evidence of an intrusion, you first need to consider what a hacker is likely to do. That way, you know what you should be looking for.

Countermeasures look for patterns that could signal an attack. They will do this by checking network packets, log files and sometimes even the memory of a program. If they detect that a hacker has been active, they can cut off access to the system and repair the damage to files by using the backup. Then the vulnerability that was exploited should be identified and a fix created.

Countermeasures and the Hacker

If you are the hacker, countermeasures can destroy all your hard work. Where the hack is a one-time deal, like when you have been hired to check the security of a system, this is no big deal.

If you are acting illegally, you certainly don't want to leave tracks leading back to you as this can lead to prosecution.

So, for the hacker, gaining access to the system and effecting changes is really only just the first step in the process. For the expert hacker, avoiding detection and leaving no tracks is the ultimate goal.

If you have concealed your attack, you can continue to sniff out data and passwords to enable you to have even more access to the system.

How to Stay Hidden as a Hacker

Staying hidden as a hacker requires a similar technique to the one used to detect hacks – you have to get into the mind of your target. You need to think about what countermeasures they employ and how you can counteract these.

This will enable you to avoid using the exploits that are known or leaving a trail that they might be looking for. You win if you can think of something that they overlooked.

The Tools You Will Need

If you are planning on being a successful hacker, there are some basic tools that you will need to have in your arsenal. What is the first thing that a professional thief does when breaking in? They gain access by overcoming the security of the system. The first thing to do is to find the appropriate exploit code to get yourself access to the system.

The professional thief will have a range of tools that help them to avoid the security measures and tripping alarms. The careful hacker can do exactly the same thing.

We have talked about writing your own exploit code in a previous chapter. So, what is the difference between writing your own exploit tool and using an exploit program? It is like the difference between hand to hand combat and a gunfight.

Writing your own code means relying on your skills, as you would in hand-to-hand combat. These tools are not meant to be used by others and they can be effective. It is also possible to miss something. These tend to be works in progress as you are bound to keep tweaking and perfecting them. The better you understand how programming works, the more effective your tools are.

Exploit tools that you have written yourself can be used to relieve tedium by automating tasks that are boring and repetitive. Tools help you to develop your own personal skills when it comes to hacking.

An exploit program, on the other hand is more like a gun. It is a complete system for exploitation and it can be used by more than one person. It is simple and easy to use and is generally a complete program. All that is required of you is to point it in the right direction and launch it.

Altering the Log Files

One of the easiest ways to erase details of your attack are to erase the log files. If you have access to administer privileges and can access a root shell, this is something that is easily done.

The catch is that this will not be possible with all systems. With more secure networks, log files are normally sent through to a different, more secure server every time they are updated. This means that, even if you delete the logs on your target computer, there will still be a record of the attack, conveniently time-and-date stamped.

There are a few techniques that you can employ to alter the log files and delete the signs that they were tampered with.

Using Meterpreter to Clear the Event Logs

You will need to most up to date version of the meterpreter in Metasploit. You will be using a script within this to cover your tracks. The script you need is known as clearev and it will delete all of the event logs.

This is something that is easily picked up by a system administrator so we are relying here on them not be vigilant.

The benefit is that it will erase the attempt to hack the system and details about your own connection. These are not the only logs that contain evidence of the attack – the IDS and router logs will as well – but this is the most important log for now.

Start off by hacking the system that you want to, using the same steps that we went through when discussing Penetration Testing. From there, you need to pull up meterpreter.

Once that is running on your system, you enter the command "meterpreter" followed by a space, the ">" sign, another space and then "clearev".

Launch Clearev and, once it has finished running, you will have cleared all the application, security and system logs on the targeted computer.

Clearing the Event Logs in a Machine Running Windows

This requires that you download a file called clearlogs.exe.

You will again need to be working within your targeted system. When in the system, all you need to do is to install clearlogs and then run it to clear the logs you want cleared.

You would type in the command "clearlogs.exe" followed by a space and then "-sec" to clear out the security logs.

This will clear any trace that you were there in the security log. You can check this by going into the Event Viewer and checking the events under the Security tab.

It is also important to remove the clearlog.exe program from the targeted system before you do sign out because this in itself will enable them to see that their system was hacked.

Clearing Up Event Logs on a Machine Running Linux

When it comes to a Linux machine, you will have to access the directory called /var/log. You can then find the text file within the directory that store the log messages. You then need to open it with a program that can edit text.

All that you need to do is to delete the log entries pertaining to your hack. This can be time-consuming and, if you don't have the time, you can just delete all the entries. Deleting all the entries will indicate quite clearly that the system has been hacked though.

Deleting your Command History

This again is for a Linux system, you will also need to make sure to erase the command history. That way, even if your attack is detected, it will be difficult for the administrator to track exactly what it is that you did.

Alternatively, change the HISTSIZE command to nil before you get started and the system is not going to even store the history in the first place. This is more efficient than going in and having to delete the history later.

Destroy Your History File

If time is very short and you have no time to either change your HISTSIZE or clear out the history, you can choose to use the shred command to overwrite the command history file. This first overwrites everything using zeros before deleting it permanently.

Making the Attack Seem Normal

If you cannot change the log files, you can sometimes get around this by changing what is logged.

A normal log file will often contain a number of different but equally valid log entries. Exploits that are executed are likely to be really easy to spot because they are short.

So basically, you want to disguise your attempt as a web request that is valid.

Chapter 8

A Little About Cryptography

When it comes to the art of hacking, cryptography becomes something that should be of great interest to you. In the digital age, a lot of information is encrypted in order to keep it safe.

The idea is that, even if you do get your hands on the information that someone is trying to keep secure, you will need to take an extra step to decrypt it so you can actually make use of it.

In order to decrypt the information, you will need the encryption key or to break the encryption. This is not always that easy.

Encryption and the Net

Once reserved for spy movies, the idea of encoding your messages has now become an extremely important consideration. You should always assume that someone is out there looking to get their hands on your personal information. There are many sniffing programs that do this online all the time.

It may sound a bit paranoid but you're not actually paranoid if someone is out to get you. And you must assume that they are.

Most transactions and sites online are protected by Secure Sockets Layer encryption. (SSL for short.) Without this your personal details when paying for something online are up for grabs. That is why it is so important to ensure that the site that you are shopping at uses SSL encryption.

In fact, Google has started taking SSL security so seriously now that it warns you upfront if a site is unsecured.

It is not only financial information that is at risk. Proprietary information is also something that needs to be protected.

Online encryption has come a long way since the early days and there are some very strong encryption programs out there now. Decrypting information that is securely encrypted is difficult – the size of the encryption key usually means that to crack it you need a lot more processing power than most of us have access to. Even if you have the processing power, decrypting the information can take a long-time due to the complexity of the cipher and the number of possible permutations.

For your own purposes, encrypting sensitive information that is stored on your own computer can be a good security procedure in case you get hacked.

For the hacker, the lure of cryptology is in that there is a puzzle to solve and this can be enticing all on its own.

Cryptography can be useful for the hacker trying to avoid being detected as well. If you are using an encrypted channel to launch your attack, automated detection measures may well prove useless.

I am going to leave the subject of cryptography there for now. To examine it fully would fill several books on its own. I do urge you to look into it and see whether or not it might be something that will interest you in the long run.

Even if you don't intend to put it into practical use in your hacking, code-breaking can prove to be an extremely interesting hobby.

Chapter 9

Putting Your New Skills to Use

Now that you have learned a bit about how to hack a system and how to cover your tracks, you are ready to move on to putting this information to use. Hacking systems can be done for many different reasons and not all of these are legal.

As mentioned before, you can stay on the right side of the law and still make a living as a hacker by offering penetration testing services. You will need to get the permission of the system owner before trying to hack any system or the act of hacking will be considered illegal. This applies even in cases where no damage was done and no information was stolen.

Here are some of the things that you might find useful as a hacker:

A Keylogger

This is software that can easily be found online or written yourself. It records the strokes you make on your keyboard in sequence and stores them in a special log. This log is relayed to the hacker or recovered by them.

The goal of the keylogger is to find out what the usernames and passwords used on the targeted systems are. This is why many banks have started to use virtual keyboards.

This doesn't need to be in the form of a program on the system either. You can also get a KeySweeper. This looks like a charger with a USB connection and will keep a record of everything typed on the keyboard. The KeySweeper is then retrieved to gain access to the information.

If you are using a public terminal, it is a good idea to check that there are no USB devices plugged in anywhere. It is also a good idea to do the same thing with computers at work that others have had access to.

It is safer not to use public terminals for personal business at all wherever possible.

Denial of Service

We have covered these briefly already. The aim here is to disable the target system's server or site by overwhelming it with so much traffic that it is unable to cope. The system then crashes.

Zombie computers or botnets are often used in these kinds of attacks. Their sole purpose being to constantly send request packets to the targeted system.

Waterhole attacks

This is where you go in and attack the targeted system where it is most easily accessed. (In much the same way that predators often stalk their prey when they are drinking water. The prey is at a disadvantage during that stage.)

So, let's say that you need close access to the targeted system in order to be able to hack it – maybe to gain access to the same Wi-Fi signal it is using and hack that. You need to be fairly close to do this.

Getting into the person's home or office building can be problematic. But what about when they are out for lunch or coffee?

An alternative for the hacker would be to set up a fake Wi-Fi hotspot. Your target will connect to it thinking it is the one that they normally use and then you are able to gain access to their system. You can redirect them to a dummy site that will look very similar to one that they usually visit so that you gain access to their passwords and their personal data.

But what if all they do is to check social media while having coffee? Think about it for a second, how much information about you does Facebook, for example, have? This is key reconnaissance for the hacker and social media accounts package up personal information in a very nice little package.

Eavesdropping

This is more passive in nature in that the hacker is just monitoring the system. You do no harm at all here – the aim is to gather information. This is a particularly dangerous data collecting method for the target system as they may never even realize that they are being monitored.

This also leaves very little in the way of tracks in the system itself.

Phishing

As a hacker, you have to get the information about someone's username and passwords in some manner or another. This can be done by setting up a fake version of a site that the person you are hacking often goes onto and then getting them to visit the site.

The fake site must look very much like the real site and you have to give people a good reason to click on the fake link. This is often done by telling them that they need to confirm their access details to the bank, that someone has tried to hack their account and they need to reset their password. Another favorite is to tell them they are due for a tax refund.

Once on the site, they log in and a trojan that you have installed on this site will record the details that they input.

Virus, Trojan etc.

These are spread from computer to computer and need to be installed in order to work. This can be as a result of you hacking the system and installing the program. A far simpler way is to get the unsuspecting user to open a file containing the Trojan or virus.

These programs might be designed to read personal data and transmit it back to you. They can also be designed to create chaos on the targeted system. These types of files are usually easily transmitted from one user to the next.

Spyware

Spyware is used for the intent purpose of gathering information and transmitting it back to you as the hacker. Good spyware does not damage the system it is installed on because the goal is to collect as much information as possible.

Malware

These programs are nasty and should not be employed by the ethical hacker at all. They may be designed to gather information but, in the end, they will also destroy files, data, etc.

Clickjacking Attacks

This is where you as the attacker hijacks the links that the target clicks on and redirects them to a different page than what they thought they were going through to.

Cookie Theft

Cookies on a browser store our personal access details, including usernames and passwords. The idea is that it makes it easier for us to sign in to our sites the next time.

This is a wealth of information and if you as a hacker can gain access to it, you have all the passwords and usernames you need.

Bait and Switch

This is where you use a copy of a legitimate program and install malicious code into it. The user thinks that they are getting the legitimate program and install the software. When they do this, you can have full access to their system.

The program may seem exactly the same as the legitimate program but your code runs in the background.

<u>Conclusion</u>

So now we have taken you a few steps further along your hacking journey. You now have even more skills to use to help you take advantage of systems that may be at risk.

How you use this knowledge is completely up to you. If you do want to progress in the art of hacking, however, you are going to need to get some practice.

If you don't feel confident enough to hack someone else's system, you can simply set up a virtual computer to practice on.

Explore Kali Linux and see what else you are able to do with it. The world beyond Windows is quite an exciting one to explore.

Have fun and enjoy the freedom of truly being able to look behind the curtain.

Book Three Starts Here

Tor

Accessing The Deep Web & Dark Web With

Tor: How To Set Up Tor, Stay Anonymous

Online, Avoid NSA Spying & Access The Deep

Web & Dark Web

Jack Jones

Table of Contents

Introduction

The technological advances that we as a society have made in the last few decades have been mind-boggling. I remember my mother telling me that when she was a child, her father told her man would never set foot on the moon. And now, there are plans in place to colonize Mars!

When we look at all the advancements made, the internet has to take top place when it comes to the development that has had the biggest impact on us as a society.

From very humble beginnings in what was essentially a messaging system, the net has grown into a giant, media rich network with the ability to connect every person on the face of the earth.

You can find out everything about a person if you know where to look. All of our data, photos, videos, etc. in the personal and business arenas are out on the web.

And the scary part is that a lot of this data is collected without your knowledge. The sites you surf, the searches you do, cookies you install, etc. all allow a very accurate picture of what your preferences are. This is why Google and Facebook show you ads related to things that you may very well be interested in – they know what you're looking for.

So, it's not just the bad guys that you have to look out for. You no doubt try to protect your personal information from those who would use it to rip you off – such as being careful when you your credit card to pay for goods online, etc.

But not everyone who is looking for information on you is trying to steal from you. Granted, they do still want your money, but this is because they want to sell you something.

Are you really happy with this kind of free-for-all when it comes to your personal information?

I, for one, am not. But for the average web user it can be tough to get around this. Every single time you make use of an application on the web or a piece of software, they expect you to agree to their terms upfront.

What most people don't know, however, is that part of these terms is to make your personal data available to the developer.

Google, for example, knows where you live, where you are hanging out, what you are looking to buy, etc. Every time you run a Google search, it is collecting more information on you.

And it is all perfectly legal. Besides which, what can you do about it anyway?

Well, one alternative is to switch up your search engine to one such as DuckDuckGo. This is a different kind of search engine because it does not collect or store your personal information at all.

For most users, however, Google will always be the go-to search engine. For starters, the risk of losing too much personal data is managed and most of those using the internet couldn't care less.

If you've been online for a while, you have no doubt had something hacked. Maybe your Facebook account, maybe your website. Maybe it was just bad luck and you ran into some top-shelf hacker who was able to break through every firewall until they gained access. After all, it wasn't your fault, was it?

I hate to break it to you, but a hacker with the skills to hack any system they want would be on to bigger and better things – they are not interested in posting porn on your Facebook page.

For the most part, most of us are small-fry that are not worth the hacker's trouble.

There are some exceptions, of course, but we'll go into that later.

If, however, you do lose your hard-earned cash to a hacker online, the chances are that you made a stupid mistake like failing to log off your Facebook when using a shared PC or choosing a password that is easy to guess.

I once hacked my mom's Facebook because it was so easy to do considering she had chosen such a simple password. The scary part is that anyone who had seen her posts on Facebook would have been able to do the same.

This section here is not about victim-shaming, please don't get me wrong. All I am trying to do is to illustrate a point – most of the time, a hack is as a result of a mistake that you have made.

But stop worrying about it – this book has been designed to make you the ultimate covert operative online. We are going to plug the information leaks and let you surf to your heart's content without giving away all your personal details.

Now, there are many ways to do this, so many, in fact, that we could write a whole series of encyclopedias on the topic. So I will concentrate on just one for this book – TOR, The Onion Routine Project.

This was initially developed for military use but is now open to all.

It puts new meaning to the phrase "incognito" when surfing the web. When used properly, TOR can help you keep your private information to yourself when surfing the web.

Are you ready to add some layers of protection?

Chapter 1

Staying Anonymous on the Deep Web

TOR is one of the solutions to keeping your personal data secure on the deep web. Let's have a look at why it's a workable solution.

This application was initially developed as a secure military communications network. Now, however, TOR servers are available to anyone online. This system protects your identity by have several routers that move traffic.

If someone runs a search on who you are, they will come up with a batch of TOR servers at random, getting them no closer to who you actually are.

The reason that the traffic is moved as it is, is so that the various nodes within the network are able to hide the person actually online – you.

This will enable you to remain anonymous in the face of the various services used to track the personal data of users.

Chapter 2

What is TOR?

So we understand basically that TOR helps you to stay anonymous and we know that it is essentially a communications network. To understand it more fully, we need to understand what it is used for as well.

What is TOR Used For?

TOR can prove to be a very handy tool. These are some of the reason why you might want to use it:

- Maybe you want to look for information that you are not meant to be looking for and need to stay anonymous.

- Maybe you need to use a shared PC and don't want to risk your data being compromised.

- Maybe you want to keep ISPs, advertisers, websites, etc. from tracking your online activity for marketing purposes.

- Maybe you want to work around the police or you are in a country that won't allow freedom of access to all information on the web.

- Perhaps you need to get your message out there without fear of recriminations.

Great, But How Does it Work?

The best analogy is an onion here. An onion is made up of a number of different layers. Each one protecting the layer beneath it. You need to work your way through these various layers in order to get to the core of the onion.

In TOR, the "layers" are the routers within the network and those wanting to find the information at the core must work their way through each of these layers.

Let's put it another way. Let's say that you need to ship a vase. You do not want it to be scratched or damaged, so you cover it with bubble wrap. You want more protection so you add a couple more layers. Then you put it into a box and place packing peanuts in there as an extra layer of protection.

The vase is very well protected. No one looking at the box would be able to see what was inside because of how it was packed. Even if someone did get to open the box and managed to take the vase out, they still couldn't see it because of the bubble wrap. Until someone persists in unwrapping each layer of bubble wrap, they are not able to see the full picture at all.

This is pretty the principle around which TOR was created. In this case, though, the vase is your data and your search history. To prevent the information being easy to track, TOR sends it through several nodes on its network. Each redirection of the traffic is like adding another layer of bubble wrap.

Nodes can consist of servers and routers worldwide and so the information can be passed on endlessly if need be.

It sounds pretty simple and it is. And the great news is that you don't have to be a techie to get the system to work for you.

Is it Secure?

It's a funny thing – this is always the first thing that I get asked. The truth is that nothing online, like in life, is ever going to be completely secure. You could run off and live in a cave to try and escape risk and get bitten on the toe by a scorpion.

TOR is also not 100% secure. Whilst it has proven to be an alternative that outperforms several others, there have been a number of weaknesses that have been found in the last few years. I have given the lists of exploits involving TOR. (These are items that hackers make use of to exploit weaknesses in a system.)

Exploits Involving TOR

- **AS Eavesdropping**: It is possible to spy on the traffic that moves into and out of the network. If the hacker is a pro, they could use this info to find out where you are.

- **Exit Node Eavesdropping**: This is the point at which the data exits the system – where the TOR hands it off to a server outside of the network. So, if you are using the TOR network to sign into a password protected server outside the network, a sophisticated hacker could get their hands on passwords or other sensitive data. It is best to use normal networks to check your emails, internet banking, etc. Avoid anything that is password protected on TOR unless it also resides on the TOR network.

- **Traffic Analysis Attack**: This is not such a huge threat but there is a chance that someone could get information about what you are doing. They should not be able to identify you though.

- **TOR Exit Node Block**: There are certain sites that will not allow users on the TOR network to fully access their sites without providing identification. Wikipedia is one such site – you can still view the information but won't be able to edit any of the pages.

- **Bad Apple Attack**: This makes use of services within the TOR that are already weak. This includes BitTorrent clients. The way a around this is simple – don't try to use TOR as a way of keeping downloads via Torrent sites anonymous.

- **Any protocol that might expose your IP address**: It's not just BitTorrent that jeopardizes your online anonymity, P2P tracker comms can also make you vulnerable. Steer clear of anything that might leave your IP address exposed.

- **Sniper Attacks**: There is very little nothing worse than an attack that leads to a denial of service. This can be done by a sophisticated hacker. They force you to use a particular set of exit nodes by blocking most nodes in the system. This allows them to figure out who you are but it is not something that amateur hackers are usually able to do.

- **Vulnerabilities with Bio Trackers**: User bio trackers can prove to be a liability within a TOR network.

- **Volume of Data**: If someone is tracking you, it is possible for them to match your activity within the TOR network by the volume of data that you are using and moving.

- **To Be Advised**: There are no doubt going to be new exploits and vulnerabilities identified as time goes on. It's not feasible to expect a system to be 100% secure all the time.

I realize that this list may make you want to think twice about the security of using the Tor network but it should be noted that there are security issues with any system. However, It should be noted that the main benefit derived from the TOR is that you can surf the web anonymously. With some additional safeguards in place, you can increase your security within the system as well.

Using TOR

Using TOR is not that hard but you do need to use a browser that will work with it. You can check the TOR Project site to get the newest releases of the tool. It is worth looking into using the TOR Project browser because it offers a simple entry to anonymous surfing.

Alternatively, you can choose to add it to your existing browser if it is compatible. Mozilla is a browser that is supported and one that you might be interested in if you are already a Mozilla user. You don't have quite as much functionality as you would have with the actual TOR browser but this is an easy option if you are not all that clued up on computers. It is as simple as adding the option to Mozilla.

The Advantages and Disadvantages of the TOR Browser

The Advantages:

- If you want the best when it comes to anonymity, it is tough to beat the browser. If you need to be able to stay private most of the time online, this is a good option. You can browse sites without leaving a trail.

- Gaining access to the Dark Web. There is a lot going on in the Dark Web. It is a zone that search engines fear to enter. It may seem enticing but it is a place where a lot of illegal deals take place. This is the place on the web where you are most likely to find things such as child pornography, murder for hire, etc. Tread lightly if you venture there because you could end up in trouble with the law.

- You'll be practically invisible to prying eyes. Your basic entry-level hacker is not going to be able to pick you up. That is not to say that you are completely safe though. A more experienced hacker might be able to find you.

- The TOR is a golden standard if you want to browse in private. It is highly mobile and allows for access to be carefully hidden.

The Disadvantages:

- If you are a stickler for performance, this is not for you. Things have been improving but it is still quite a bit slower than normal browsing. You need to decide if the increase in privacy is worth sacrificing a bit of speed.

- You won't be completely secure and you could be monitored. It should be kept in mind that state agencies monitor online activity that attempts to remain hidden. If you stumble onto a site related to illegal activities even just once, they will be monitoring you. If you are a repeat customer, they may become very interested in you. That said, don't panic too much if you find an illegal site in error. As long as you act in the correct way, you will be okay. That means that you need to get off the site as quickly as possible or make a report about the site to the relevant authorities. If you do get asked questions, be open and honest with your answers.

- There have been issues with people misusing the network because of the anonymity it provides. Reputationally, the TOR network has taken a beating. That said, not all of the activity deemed illegal is wrong. For example, many activists living in societies where there is a lot of censorship have made use of the TOR network to get their message across.

- Latency issues abound on the TOR network. You are going to need to suck it up and be patient here or avoid using this network altogether.

The Advantages and Disadvantages of the Mozilla Add-On

If you decide to go for the Mozilla add-on instead, here is what you can expect.

- Mozilla products are all free and open-source and anyone can help to improve them. The developers have ensured that people are easily able to check that the system does deliver what it claims to. Transparency helps keep the developers honest.

- You can customize the add-on as you like. That means that you can have a browsing experience that is set to your own specifications.

- You do get access to a very supportive community. For a beginner, this is most important. You can get access to assistance from various members of the community.

- Mozilla works across a range of platforms and will work with many different operating systems. If you upgrade your device in future, you are able to enjoy continuity of service because of this – you don't have to go and learn a whole new software version again.

- In addition, the add-on is constantly being improved upon. It supports HTML5, allows you to sync your data across different devices, let's you set up and manage bookmarks and has a function that allows for the quick grab of pages. It features a lower drain on your computer's resources in terms of CPU usage and memory.

- One annoyance is that you need to restart the system with every new extension that you install.

- The speed of operations is not consistent over all operating systems. It is slower when using a Mac than it would be in Linux or Windows.

- The speed at which Mozilla is being developed could end up leaving the extension behind. Extensions may not continue to work with newer versions of the browser.

Chapter 3

Will TOR work for you?

It is not always appropriate to use the TOR network. You need to draw the line between maintaining safety and anonymity online. The TOR network is not perfect and is very much still a work in progress.

And whilst the protocol underlying the TOR remains unbroken, the fact that you have to use it within a browser introduces a level of vulnerability. And browsers are not great a strong link in the chain of internet security.

Your browser is what allows you to connect with the network online but it can be exploited. It has been said that certain government agencies are able to identify and track users of the TOR network.

What that essentially means is that using the TOR system is not going to completely protect you if you want to hide illegal activity. It might make things harder on the authorities trying to find you but it won't stop them forever.

That means that illegal usage of this system is not recommended. In fact, if you have nefarious intentions, you should steer well clear of the system – if someone else in the community finds you, they are bound to report you to maintain the integrity of the online community using the network.

Avoid doing the following when on the TOR network:

- Trying to download big files if you want to retain anonymity. You will need to use some kind of torrent client and this will make it easy to track what you have downloaded. It will take longer than normal and slow the network down for everyone. And there really is nothing to gain from it.

- Trying to avoid being surveilled by a government agency. The federal government agencies are able to access the network and identify users. You are not really anonymous to them, even on the TOR network.

- Trying to stay safe online while accessing your social media accounts. The very act of accessing your social media means that you have to move off the TOR network and lose anonymity anyway. Furthermore, your access details will be exposed when you leave the network. It is not safe to surf sites that you need password access to on the TOR network.

- Accessing official websites or system. Every such access is logged and can be traced. Most people trying to access such sites are doing so for nefarious reasons. In addition to which, it is an offence to attempt unauthorized access to any site and you are risking some serious jail time if you are caught. It might be tempting,

considering how anonymous you feel but this is
not what TOR was originally designed for.

- There are lots of reasons to use the TOR
  network but you do need to bear in mind that
  the very fact that you are using an anonymous
  service like this will raise red flags for law
  enforcement agencies.

Chapter 4

Your Step By Step Guide to Getting Started with TOR

Right, are you ready to start?

Is TOR for You?

We've been through the fact that TOR will not be a good fit for everyone. The first step anyone should take is to ensure that TOR is really going to work for you.

We are not going to go through a list of pros and cons, though. We are going to look at best practices that you may need to implement if you want to use TOR.

Changing the Operating System

Windows is meant to be easy to use, even for the most unskilled user. A problem with this approach is that it is also a lot easier to hack. There are many exploits out there designed specifically around Windows.

And remember, TOR only protects your identity, it does not make your system more secure. It could pay you to change over to an operating system that is more secure, such as Linux. Linux works well with TOR.

You will also find that Mac has better security than windows and also works with TOR. Just keep in mind that the TOR network is usually slower for Mac users.

Stay Up to Date

Yes, I know those endless updates are extremely annoying but you must ensure that your operating system, browser and anti-virus programs are regularly updated. Every update has been put in place for a reason – and it could be a security reason.

HTTPS Everywhere

How many sites have you been on that don't offer HTTPS? These sites are not properly encrypted and could be dangerous to visit. An add-on for your browser known as "HTTPS Everywhere" can solve that problem for you by switching to the encrypted version of the site, where it is supported.

Data Encryption

It seems rather silly to go to all the trouble of surfing anonymously if you do not benefit in terms of increased security as well. If you are running a Linux system, you can look for TrueCrypt and LUKS to encrypt your data for you.

TOR Bundle is Not the Best Idea

It might seem as though TOR Bundle puts together the best in anonymity and security but this is a misperception that could cost you dearly.

The bundle does offer an additional layer but the FBI has pointed out that there are vulnerabilities here as well. It is best not to rely on TOR Bundle for all your security.

No More Java, Java Script and Flash

The problem with these scripts is that they could be sharing your information without any consideration about whether it is what you want to do or not. Turn these off so that your private browsing history is not shared.

No More Peer-to-Peer

Yes, I have said this a few times now. But I really want to stress the importance of this – when using this type of connection, you are potentially putting your information at risk.

Be a Cookie Monster

Cookies are in place to monitor your behavior on a particular site and store personal data. If you want to be truly anonymous, install an add-on such as Self-Destructing Cookies. These add-ons will delete the cookies.

Use Fake Accounts

You go to all the trouble of installing TOR, changing your operating system and deleting cookies as you go, and then you use your real email address. Congratulations, you have now just announced to everyone who you are. Set up a fake email account to use while in the TOR network.

Bye Bye Google

You know when they say, "Big brother is watching", they might as well be referring to Google. Google is one of the worst offenders when it comes to collecting data about you personally. Rather use a search engine that does not collect data such as StartPage or DuckDuckGo.

Act Legally

Be sure to stick to the rules when surfing anonymously. State and federal law enforcement agencies monitor anonymous users and are quick to act when illicit activities are flagged. Steer clear of sites that are less than legal.

There are some instances, however, when it is wiser to use TOR when conducting "illegal" activities. If, for example, you are living in a country where the media is heavily censored and you want to keep an eye on international media without being monitored.

Choose Whether to Use the TOR Browser or an Add-On

So now you have made your decision – you have decided that TOR will work well for you.

We have been through the advantages and disadvantages of either course of action and so you have no doubt made a decision as to which is the preferred option for you. Who knows, maybe you've decided that you'll make use of both.

Stepping Behind the Curtain

You are almost ready to step inside TOR. First of all, make sure that you have physically logged out of any applications that you have on your system. If you do not do this, you run the risk of them sharing your data whilst in TOR.

Once you have done that, where do you start to explore? Here are some suggestions.

Hidden Wiki

This is the TOR version of Wikipedia. You can use it to find items that you are interested in. This site lists what hidden onion sites there are and lists what topics are covered. To find Hidden Wiki is simple – just access your DuckDuckGo search engine to search for it. You'll find it quite easily that way.

What you could find:

- **News**: Getting uncensored news is one of the primary, more legitimate uses of TOR. You are able to find all the most up to date news. There are several sites within the TOR network devoted to giving up to date news. All you need to do is to find one that is credible and that is of interest to you.

- **Introduction Points**: These can be considered stepping stones. They bridge the gap between the "normal" web and the TOR sites. These will be the first sites that you come across within the network.

- **Commercial Services**: There are going to be times when you want to buy something completely anonymously. Bitcoins can be used here and this makes it possible for transactions to be conducted entirely anonymously. The transactions can be traced but it will take someone with excellent skills to do so when you are within the TOR network.

- **History**: Despite what you may have been taught in school, history can be more a matter of perspective than of actual fact. As they say, history is in the hands of the winners. If, for example, the Nazis had won World War II, what would we have been taught of the Holocaust today? Searching through TOR, you are more likely to find actual personal accounts, etc. that have not been spun to look good.

- **Forums**: Are you desperate to discuss how bad your government is but scared of recriminations? You could join an online community within the TOR system. Google, etc. has similar forums but it is not nearly as easy to remain anonymous with these. The developers of these forums on the normal web have full access to your IP address, real user name and email address (even if these are hidden from the rest of the community) and they can be compelled to hand that information over.

- **Dangerous Topics**: The anonymity of the TOR system is obviously a huge drawcard for those who are conducting illicit activities. There are many sites that will teach you how to create viruses, how to hack systems, create malware, etc. It is better to steer clear of these sites to avoid getting into trouble with the authorities. This may be difficult to do as some of these sites will pop-up on your screen. If you do come across them by accident or by pop-up, don't get drawn in - you just need to close them as quickly as possible.

For most uses, however, the Hidden Wiki is going to give you all the information that you need. The lists on the site may not always be current but it is still the best source of information about what is on the TOR network.

Sites within the TOR network are not always maintained or as long-lasting as those outside of the network.

It is a good idea to set up bookmarks when you find a site that you want to visit again. Unlike the normal web, URLS on the TOR network are difficult to remember. In addition, you cannot always rely on the directories within the Hidden Wiki either. This might mean having to do some serious searching to find a site again. Bookmark it to be on the safe side.

Onion Chat

Onion Chat refers to anonymous chat rooms on the TOR network. Because of the anonymity aspect, they are more likely to remain in service for longer. You can even make friends during these chats.

That said, however, it should always be a priority to guard your identity – use a nickname and never reveal information about yourself that could let them figure out who you are. It would be unwise to tell someone which town you live in, where you work, etc.

New Yorker Strongbox

News agencies often rely on insider information when it comes to blowing scandals wide open. The New Yorker maintains a site on the TOR network to allow people who want to give them tips to do so completely anonymously. They assign you a code name and never force you to reveal who you actually are. (Though, if you are hoping to get paid, you will have to reveal this at some stage.)

It Can be Lonely In the TOR

TOR is not a network that everyone knows about and it is not someone that everyone knows how to use. There is a sense of being alone on the network because those who have sites and blogs may not make regular posts.

Users of TOR are looking for anonymity and so may not want to interact with you. In addition, websites within the network tend to be of a more transient nature.

Unlike the normal web, there is not going to be someone trying to sell you something every five minutes and finding information is not necessarily going to be quick and easy.

Knowing that upfront means that you understand that you have to exercise patience and be more resourceful than usual. The latency problems with the system can also cause a lot of irritation.

It is the tradeoff that you make for being able to surf anonymously.

Best Practices

Here we will go through what you can do to get the most out of using TOR on a regular basis, especially when it comes to navigating the system and communicating within it.

Browsing Safely

TOR will not connect with Google by design. What it does is to connect to a page that basically interacts with Google on your behalf. This prevents Google from being able to make logs of whatever you have searched for. (Ever wonder how you always seem to see ads that are so on point after Googling something?

Google makes notes of what you search for and ensures that it displays ads related to your search preferences.)

Because the TOR network puts this page in between you and Google, Google is not able to attribute the search to any particular person. It makes it impossible to trace by simple means accessible to most users. (Not counting governmental agencies, of course.)

Where TOR cannot do anything is when it comes to the sites, scripts and any extensions that are run. If you are using the TOR browser, it will disable information-gathering scripts, etc. by default. It is not a good idea to mess with this default setting at all or you risk exposing your identity.

It should also be realized that, due to the privacy settings, some applications may not run as well as they should. For example, Flash protocols are disabled on the TOR network and so you might not be able to watch your favorite YouTube channel, for example.

Some streaming of YouTube has been made possible with the HTML5 additions YouTube has made but this is still in the early stages.

Where TOR does excel, however, is in warning you which files or documents might compromise your identity. And it tends to be pretty accurate so it is best to take such warnings to heart.

Anonymous Messaging

When it comes to the normal web, anonymous messaging is impossible. Even if you are using nicknames, all your personal information, including your IP address, etc. is on record with the company offering the service.

In addition, all messaging services log your chats and monitor them. Which essentially means that nothing is really private anymore.

That's where making use of the TOR system can also be very effective. TorChat is a messaging app that can be used as a simple extension. All you need to do is to download the app from the site and run the executable file to install it.

The app works exactly as your normal messaging programs do and is very user-friendly. The primary difference is that you are assigned a name by the system that consists of a random number of characters.

You are able to assign nicknames to people on your list so that you know who you are speaking to.

And, because the system runs on the TOR network, it is not possible to easily trace your real identity, nor will anyone else be able to establish who you are speaking to.

Crypto Messaging

Should you want to go all 007 here, you can also encrypt your messages and then send them through the TOR network.

The problem here is that there is a greater chance that the messages can be intercepted because the apps that allow encryption won't work in the background. However, because the messages are encrypted, anyone who intercepts them will find them difficult to read. A service like Cryptocat is a good option here and it can be downloaded from the Cryptocat site.

Emails That are Truly Anonymous

What happens when instant messages are no good? What if you must send an email? The TOR network does have a hidden email service but you have to be within the network to make use of it.

In order to access it, you just need to go to the site while on the TOR network and set it up from there.

The service is very user-friendly and intuitive to use. It looks similar to your usual online mail clients. The big advantage is that it is impossible to access it or search through the messages unless you are in the TOR network.

Step-by-Step Guide to TOR

Go to the official site and find the Browser download page. In Windows, this is quite easy – you usually just need to hit the download button and allow it to be installed. If you are running a different operating system, you should follow the developer's instructions for that system.

Here is a more technical breakdown of the process for you:

This is for those who are more technically minded and who want to run through the process one step at a time.

TOR Browser Installation with the Windows Operating System

As mentioned above, it is pretty simple to install the browser into windows.

1. Close all programs other than your web browser.

2. Start at the official TOR website and look for the updated version of the browser. On the top right-hand side of the screen you will see a tab for Downloads. Click on this.

3. Now select the operating system you are using. The options you can choose from include Apple, Window, Source Code, Smartphones and Linux so you can download it to your laptop, tablet or smartphone – or all of your devices if you like.

4. Select your language preference in order to begin the download. You will be given the option of also downloading TOR Bundle – a toolset aimed at making it easier to improve your privacy when you are surfing. (Just remember what I mentioned earlier about not relying solely on the TOR Bundle for this. Do take the other steps to further increase your safety while browsing.)

5. You will be asked where you want to save the actual installed files on your device. This is not a major issue as it has little effect on how the rest of the process goes. (Just ensure that you have enough memory on the device so that you can install the files.)

6. As soon as the download is complete, you can open it so that it can install the browser. If you decide to do this later on, you will need to find the files in the location that you had chosen earlier.

7. Select the appropriate language that you want to use and then press the OK button.

8. You will again need to choose where the files will run from. Again, make sure the memory is adequate for this. (A pop-up window will come up with a suggested download path, showing how much memory is needed and how much is available. If you want it installed to a different location, hit the "Browse" button and choose the location that you want, otherwise continue as normal.)

9. Leave the installer to do its thing – this will take a few minutes.

10. You will be asked if you want to also install a link in the start menu and if you want to create a shortcut on the desktop. The decision is

yours. Once that decision is made, the browser is fully installed and ready to use.

Using TOR Through BlackBelt Privacy on Firefox

1. If you would rather use the software through Firefox, you can use BlackBelt to help you do this. You will need to have the Firefox browser as well so if you don't have it, download it now.

2. Search for BlackBelt Privacy + TOR and download the latest version. It won't take long because it's a very small file.

3. Open the file and then choose one of the following options:

TOR Client Only Operator – this enables you to use the TOR network but doesn't allow others to use you as a relay.

Bridge Relay Operator – This enables you to use the TOR network and to also act as a relay so that others can do the same.

Censored User – If you are using this to avoid censorship at home, this should be the option that you choose.

4. Once you have selected what kind of TOR user you want to be, you can carry on with installing the program.

5. As soon as it is installed, you can start browsing anonymously.

Setting it Up Manually

1. If something goes wrong and the configuration does not seem to be working as it should, you can try the following manual settings.

2. You need to have installed the TOR browser before starting, so do that now.

3. Despite the fact that we have installed the browser, we are not going to use it to navigate, we are going to use Mozilla instead. (Mozilla is updated more frequently than the TOR browser and this means improved and more up to date security.)

4. Once TOR is installed, open up your Mozilla browser and click on the settings button – you want to choose Proxy settings.

5. If you want to do the same for Windows, go to your Menu, select Options, choose Advanced Options, find Network and then go to Settings.

6. From there are the process is that same for both – you are going to manually set the proxies. Do this as follows: SOCKS Host: 127.0.0.1; Port Box: 9150 and, if given the option, choose SOCKS v5. Check that the Remote DNS box has been checked. After No Proxy for introduce: 127.0.0.1.

7. Now check if the TOR is working. If so, you will receive a message to say that you are navigating anonymously. If not, you will receive a message that your IP address is detectable.

8. If it is still not working, it is better to deactivate it completely and see if you can walk through the troubleshooting process.

How to Set Up Hidden Services

Are you intrigued by using hidden services within the TOR network? Does it sound like fun? What if you set your own up?

What is nice is that it is relatively simple to set up your very own hidden service within the TOR network.

For this to work, you must first install the TOR browser on your device.

After that, you need to set up a local server to use. According the TOR experts, Windows users should try using Savant and Max or Linux users should try using thttpd Web Server.

You can choose a different server if you like but do keep in mind that this may open you up to a different set of vulnerabilities.

Open up the configuration and select HTTP first, from there select Server DNS. Type in the word "localhost" and, where it says "Port # To Serve From" type in "80".

Your usual path for Savant in Windows is: C:\Savant\Root directory. You need to ensure that the default used by Savant is replaced by your "Index.html" document.

You can see whether or not things are running as they should by opening your browser and typing "localhost" into it.

To check that everything is running correctly, you just need to type localhost in the browser. You can use a different port if you want – set it up by entering "localhost:[#of the port]". So, you could for example, type "localhost:125 for port # 125".

You have now brought the local server up online and can set up your hidden service.

All that you need to do is to let the TOR browser know that you have set up a new server. This can be done by: Closing your TOR browser as needed; Typing "torrc" into your computer's search function (You can also look to see if it is in the Tor directory on your computer); Opening this file using a simple editor like Notepad; Adding in some text such as: # Hidden Service; HiddenServiceDir C: \Users\Name\tor_service; HiddenServicePort 80 127.0.0.1:80.

You then need to go into C:\Users\Name\tor_service string and change this to an actual path set on your computer.

You should not use a website to use as a directory here. You will have to match the final number in the new string to the port you chose earlier when setting up the local server.

If you do not have a tor_service folder, create a new folder for it. Save your changes and then restart the browser again.

You would then need to check through your message log to ensure that everything went smoothly with the configuration.

There are going to be 2 documents in the tor_service folder – private_key and hostname.

These make sure that your service functions as it should and so should be kept safe. If someone gets their hand on the key, they can use it to delete the hidden service you have set up.

If you open the hostname file, you will see the hidden address's onion address. This is what you can share with those that you want to be able to use the service.

You have now set up a TOR site and can post what you like to it. Visitors to the site will have to be on the TOR network in order to use it.

So, it really isn't too difficult to set up a service within the TOR network. You can thus post news, etc. and share as you like with other TOR users. This is a very easy way to create a website on TOR. If you want something that looks great though, you may need to learn more about CSS and HTML.

But that is something outside the scope of this book. Tutorials on creating websites abound online and so you should have no problems finding one. There are also tons of free, generic templates that can be customized to your own needs if that is what you are looking for.

Tips to Make TOR Run Better

- No Torrents or Peer-to-peer sharing. These will work a lot more slowly in TOR and so you will hold up everyone. In addition, your IP address is revealed when doing so and that kind of makes the whole anonymity aspect void.

- Disable plug-ins for the browser unless you have personally developed them. Even when working within the TOR network, if info-gathering plug-ins have been installed, they will continue to collect data about what you have been doing.

- Always use HTTPS and don't visit sites that don't support this functionality. It is the entry and exit points to the TOR system that are most likely to be problematic when it comes to keeping your identity secret. Whilst on the network, your identity is protected, but that is not the case when moving off or onto the network. You can counter this through the proper use of encryption. If you use the add-on HTTPS Everywhere, you are going to be able to further protect your information. Sites that do not support secure HTTP protocols should be avoided completely.

- Wait until after exiting the TOR network to read documents that you may have downloaded. The potential problem is that many of these documents are stored in the cloud and may need user verification to open. A click will take you to the correct page and your system may automatically log you in to Adobe Reader, for example, giving away your identity. It is best not to click on links that will open anything while on the network.

- Make use of bridges. The TOR system allows you to make use of a number or relays instead of interacting directly with sites. Be sure that you make use of these to further protect your identity while surfing.

- Get your friends to come on board. The more people that use the TOR network, the stronger it becomes. Tell people about it and the advantages of using it and get them to try it out for themselves.

Chapter 5

Where to Go and What to See on the Deep Web

I just want to preface this by saying that exploring the deep web can seem exciting but it's important to remember that some of what you will come across is highly illegal. There are some pretty sick people out there and you might come across things that you really don't want to see.

In addition, you could end up getting yourself into a lot of trouble with the law if you get involved in any of the illicit activities in the deep web. At times, such as when it comes to unintentionally viewing illicit material such as child pornography, the act of just seeing the site can get you into trouble regardless of your intentions. So, even if you are not actually intending to get involved with anything illegal on the deep web, you stand the chance of getting into trouble.

The best way to protect yourself in situations such as these is to immediately get off the site. You should also consider reporting the matter to the relevant authorities.

For your own sake, do not use the TOR network to solicit crimes or commit crimes. As I have mentioned several times before, the authorities are on the lookout for this kind of thing.

Using Hidden Services

Hidden services are regularly used within the TOR network because they add another level of privacy. Websites using such services are not subject to being spied upon in the same way as normal sites are.

This makes them less likely to be able to be blocked or spammed. They can theoretically run indefinitely because there is no way for outsiders to take them down.

Let's look at a real-world example here. Say, for example, I am annoyed with a company and I want to cause them real harm. If I could get enough people on my side, we could spam the company's site until it crashed.

It would take some effort but it would be possible to do because, on the normal internet, their servers, etc. would be fairly easy to find. It would then be a matter of throwing enough data at them to overload their capacity.

If, on the other hand, they could keep their services hidden, I would not be able to spam the site and crash it.

With the TOR network, the servers are anonymous and so less vulnerable to attack. As a result, you will be able to use the services every day. Anonymity can also be valuable to those wanting to transfer things like Bitcoins in secret.

Making Use of Bookmarks

Where all the anonymity can become annoying is when you want to find a site that you have visited before. Sites on the TOR network don't have a typical URL. You are not going to find something like Amazon.com. Instead, you will find something more along the lines of armjagsgdgada.onion.

That makes it pretty hard to remember the address of sites that you have visited. In addition, the pages within the deep web are not indexed as normal web pages are so keyword searches are not as helpful.

Finding a site then might actually depend more on luck. If you do find a site that you'll want to visit again, bookmark it. You can always delete the bookmark later if you want to.

Finding Information in the Deep Web

We've already spoken a bit about Hidden Wiki as a means of finding sites of interest in the deep web. The Hidden Wiki does, however, share only information that is considered safe for general consumption.

TorSearch is another way to find information.

It works similarly to Google except that it doesn't track your personal searches. It has also made it a lot easier to find things in the deep web.

Issues that You May Encounter

Anonymity is one thing. Online security is something else. When using the TOR network you run the risk of being exposed to vulnerabilities. Experienced hackers may still be able to track you.

In addition, you might also be exposing yourself to viruses – after all, not everyone using the deep web is there with good intentions, are they?

You also need to assume that you are being monitored when using the TOR network. Whilst it may be harder for normal people to track you, governmental agencies are able to do so. And are more likely to do so because you are using the network. This means that you have to be really careful about what sites you click on.

Being Careful in the Deep Web

There are some search engines that are available in the deep web but you do need to be circumspect about which you choose.

For example, there is a search engine called Grams that has garnered a lot of interest from authorities because of its relation to drugs and online dealing of the same.

There are several online markets within the TOR network as well. These include Agora, Middle Earth and Evolution to name but a few.

Middle Earth tends to be more user-friendly. Evolution and Agora, on the other hand, tend to be more reliable and this makes them a more popular choice.

It is very important, before you make any kind of purchase within the TOR network that you understand exactly how it is going to work. You also need to understand the possible implications of buying what it is that you are buying, especially if it is of an illegal nature.

When it comes to paying for goods, one thing you never want to do here is to give anyone your personal information. You can get around this by using Bitcoins. For this you will need a Bitcoin wallet and to purchase Bitcoins. This can be done on the official Bitcoin site.

Bitcoins are a cryptocurrency and are the safest way to exchange money in the TOR network.

It can be just as tough making a decision about whether or not a site is trustworthy as it is on the normal internet. Look for references from other clients before completing the purchase and, when in doubt, don't go through with it.

Concerns About Content

Because of the nature of the content in the TOR network, a general web search can be more of a risk than a normal web search would be.

Here are some of the things that you have to look out for in the TOR network:

Unlinked Content: There is no indexing of sites by a search engine. You will not be able to find links or backlinks on the sites.

Dynamic Content: These sites will require you to have some knowledge of how domains work in order for you to access them. They might require you to send queries while navigating.

Private Webs: These are essentially membership sites. You need to be circumspect about such sites because you will be required to give personal information in order to become a member. There are fake sites out there designed to get hold of your personal information.

Contextual Webs: These sites may require different access contexts. For example, they might place reliance on prior clients here.

Limited Access Content: Systematically these sites tend to be more difficult for search engines to index.

They have CAPTCHAs, etc. in place to ensure that they are less vulnerable to robots.

Scripted Content: These websites require the use of JavaScript or Flash software, for example. As mentioned previously, such scripts can be used to gather personal information.

Software Driven Content: You need to have the correct program or app installed to gain access here.

Web Archives: These will often let you look at previous incarnations of websites. This can be used to see what previous versions of sites were in place.

The TOR network contains many different formats online just as your normal browsing does. The key to keeping safe here is that you understand what the different formats are and how they might affect you.

Just like the regular internet, you don't want to download files that can create changes on your computer or files that you just randomly come across.

What is the Future of the Deep Web?

In the last few years, the numbers of people using the TOR network has been steadily increasing. There has also been an uptake of people trying to escape political censorship, as can be seen during the events of the Arab spring.

Activism is one large reason for resorting to the use of TOR but there has also been an uptake of people who just want to be able to experience the internet free of censorship.

The truth is though that there are unplumbed depths when it comes to the deep web. How much information there actually is, is anyone's guess.

Getting an accurate estimate to the actual amount of information is difficult because of the nature of the network itself. What is known is that the number of users has increased substantially.

It no longer takes a range of skills to be able to make use of the deep web – you can set up your own hidden services in a matter of minutes. And, if you're not sure of how to get more out of the web, you can easily consult an online tutorial.

More and more people are looking to be able to surf anonymously – whether that is in an effort to conceal illicit activities or in a misguided attempt to feel more secure online.

It should never be forgotten that as the system becomes more and more popular, it will become more of a target for hackers looking to score personal information.

There are not the normal safeguards in place – you are anonymous but that doesn't mean you are completely safe. In fact, it may be more dangerous for the uninitiated because it is so unregulated – even if you come across a scamming website, shutting it down is easier said than done.

Considering how easy it is for scammers online already, the deep web can be like the old wild west – if you're not careful, you'll end up being a victim.

You could end up being scammed because there are lots of sites out there itching to take your money. And there is little to no recourse if you do get scammed.

But, in the grand scheme of things, is it really so different in the regular online world? As long as you are aware of the potential risk, you are far better able to keep yourself safe.

It might be safer to stay out of the deep web but it's safer in the same way as it would be to never leave your home. Sure, if you don't set foot out the door, you are not likely to get hit by a bus but you're not going to have any fun either.

But, if you set out each day, aware of how to keep yourself safe, you can have new and exciting experiences.

Who's to say that the TOR network is not the next evolution in the development of the internet? Who's to say that in a few years' time we won't all crave the anonymity that came before Facebook and Twitter became such a big part of our lives?

If you told someone fifty years ago that you could have a face to face conversation with someone on the other side of the planet, they would have thought you were mad but today we have Skype and video calls.

Our grandparents would never have imagined a world where just about everything could be ordered by clicking on a few sites online. Who knows what our future will be like and who knows what role a TOR network might play in that?

Concerns About Privacy

Privacy is something that is hard to come by in the modern world. News breaks instantly across the world and is discussed many times over. In minutes news on social media and from there it spreads virally. This can be a good thing.

But, on a personal level, our own privacy has never become more precious. Social media makes it all but impossible to keep secrets anymore.

I'll cite an incident from my own life as an example. My brother and his ex-wife have a very acrimonious relationship. The same can be said of her and the rest of our family. She has blocked all members of the family from her Facebook page.

Anyway, the one weekend my nephew was visiting, I posted a picture of him on my Facebook page – only to have her comment on it. I didn't even realize she would see it and I didn't want her commenting. Now, I have since changed my privacy settings but it made it very clear that privacy has taken on a new meaning now.

Despite the fact that I was not connected to her on Facebook on a one-to-one level, she was connected through a third person and so had access to my news.

So, yes, I can understand the increased desire for privacy. I can understand why people would want to work within the TOR network.

The TOR network is a tool like any other. It can be used for good or evil, just like any other. As and of itself, it is neither good nor evil, it really depends on how you use it.

Do services like this have a future on the internet where just about everything is monitored? Yes, because people do have some desire for privacy.

Will it be misused? Of course, there are always people who will look for an easy answer.

Can it be a tool for great good? The answer, again, is yes. Think to a few years ago when Egypt cut off all access to the internet for its people. Think about countries where it is illegal to access general information because of extreme censorship.

And think of the possibilities for a low cost communication system that can truly be deemed private. Think about surfing the web without worrying about how all your personal data is being used for marketing purposes.

The internet has proven to be a source of great information and the deep web can help with this. All that is needed is to introduce some sort of regulation to it so that those misusing the system can be brought to book.

Used responsibly, the deep web is a very powerful tool.

<u>Conclusion</u>

The idea of exploring unknown territory is exciting but there is so much more that you gain from the TOR network. Designed to facilitate unfettered communication, this allows you to truly experience online freedom.

How you use that freedom is up to you but I hope that you look on this as a great opportunity.

Learning about the TOR network and having my own forays into the deep web was an eye-opening experience for me. And it was all a lot easier than I could ever have imagined.

I hope that this book has given you the confidence to explore on your own and that you are now willing to look around the deep web for yourself.

Have fun!

Check Out My Other Books!

Hacking - The Complete Beginner's Guide To Computer Hacking: How To Hack Networks and Computer Systems, Information Gathering, Password Cracking, System Entry & Wireless Hacking

Tor - Accessing The Deep Web & Dark Web With Tor: How To Set Up Tor, Stay Anonymous Online, Avoid NSA Spying & Access The Deep Web & Dark Web

Hacking & Tor - The Ultimate Beginners Guide To Hacking, Tor, & Accessing The Deep Web & Dark Web

Powershell - The Ultimate Windows Powershell Beginners Guide. Learn Powershell Scripting In A Day!

Kodi - *The Ultimate Guide To Kodi: How To Install Kodi On A Fire TV Stick, Stream Live TV, Jailbreak A Fire TV Stick, & Everything Else Kodi Related!*

Hacking - The Complete Beginner's Guide To Computer Hacking: More On How To Hack Networks & Computer Systems, Information Gathering, Password Cracking, System Entry & Wireless Hacking

PowerShell: The Ultimate Windows Powershell Beginners Guide - Part 2. Take Your Powershell Scripting Further!

Hacking: The Complete Beginners Guide To Computer Hacking: Your Guide On How To Hack Networks & Computer Systems, Information Gathering, Password Cracking, System Entry & Wireless Hacking

All books available as ebooks or printed on Amazon.
Some available as audiobook.

www.ingramcontent.com/pod-product-compliance
Lightning Source LLC
LaVergne TN
LVHW022300060326
832902LV00020B/3191